D0907605

Modern
Korean Poetry

Selected and translated
with an introduction
by
Jaihiun J. Kim

ASIAN HUMANITIES PRESS
Fremont, California

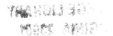

Library of Congress Cataloging-in-Publication Data

Modern Korean poetry / selected and translated with an introduction
    by Jaihiun J. Kim.
        p.   cm.
    Includes bibliographical references and index.
    ISBN 0-87573-057-4
    1. Korean poetry—20th century—Translations into English.
    I. Kim, Jaihiun, 1934-
PL984.E3M64   1994
895.7'1408—dc20   94-18319
                                                                    CIP

Contents

1930s

1940s and 1950s

1960s and 1970s

Acknowledgements

Grateful acknowledgement is made to Hanshin Publishing Company for permission to reprint large portions of poems from *Korean Poetry Today* and its Introduction.

The author also wishes to thank The Daewoo Foundation for partly subsidizing the book's publication expense.

Preface

The purpose of this anthology is to provide the reader with a bird's-eye-view of modern Korean poetry from the 1920s down to the 1980s. As is the case with many other anthologists, I have found it necessary to set a limit on the time-span. Naturally, this by no means excludes recent works of those who won recognition as poets in the earlier years. It is my belief that a historical evaluation of the achievement of the poets who have emerged in the 1980s will have to wait for the perspective of time. Incidentally, this anthology owes much to my former collections: *The Immortal Voice, Master Poems from Modern Korea* and *The Contemporary Korean Poets*. In fact, since it came out in 1974, *The Immortal Voice* has been widely used as a reference book of scholars at home and abroad. It has, however, been long out of print after the first edition. In 1980 I made the two other selections. But pressure of time and urgency of needs necessarily fell short of satisfying my original intentions. In this book I have cut off all deadwood from *The Immortal Voice* and touched up the rest, adding to it more than 150 new poems with thirty younger poets included. And with the exception of a few poets whose works were not available for one reason or another, the 88 poets represented here can as major figures stand for the significant trends in Korean poetry today.

Selection of poets has been made by the translator with helpful suggestions of Professor Kim, Yongjik at Seoul National University. For the inclusion of particular poems in this anthology, I am solely responsible. However, I have taken extreme care to draw as objective a picture as possible. As a guiding principle, I have made a point of presenting the best or the most representative pieces of each poet, the number of his work ranging from three to seven or more so that any one concerned with Korean poetry might have an in-depth access to each poet. The chronological arrangement of poets in each period is made simply for convenience.

Jaihiun Joyce Kim
Seoul, Korea 1993

Introduction

The earliest Korean poetry was written as far back as the rise of Korean civilization. "Song for Golden Orioles," the earliest extant poem, composed in Chinese characters by King Yuri (ca. 19 B.C.-17 A.D.) of the Koguryo Kingdom (ca. 3 B.C.-668 A.D.), reads as follows:

> Golden orioles are flitting about,
> Male and female enjoying each other.
> Left alone to myself in solitude,
> Who shall I return home with?*

It is obvious that volumes of poems were produced during the fourteen centuries until the end of the Koryo Dynasty (918-1392). To our great regret, however, we have left to us only 25 poems which have survived the ravages of time. *Hyang'ga*, native songs as they were called, are the poetic heritage of the Shilla Kingdom. Most of them are thematically related to Buddhism. For instance, a widow prays for the bliss of her husband's departed soul in "Song for Nirvana:"

> O moon, are you proceeding
> as far as the Western Land?
> Please go and tell Buddha
> Of Immeasurable Bliss
> that there's one poor soul left behind
> praying, her hands joined,
> before Merciful Amitabha
> that her husband may enter Nirvana.
> For herself, she only desires
> to have forty wishes come true.

The *hyang'ga*, four to ten lines in length, evolved into the *tan'ga* or the short songs, typically of three lines, in the latter part of the Koryo Dynasty. *Sijo*, an appelation given to *tan'ga* in the 18th century, settled into a fixed form as late as the mid-15th century with the invention and

---

* A story is told of the composition of the poem. King Yuri on his return home from hunting found that the more favored of his two wives had left him after a quarrel with the other. He hastened after her and pleaded with her in vain to come back. On his way back he chanced to see a couple of orioles flying about in a tree.

propagation of the Korean alphabet, *han'gul.* Surviving *sijo* poems including those written throughout the whole period of the Chosun Dynasty (1392-1910) approximately 3,600 in number. While the tradition of *sijo* poetry has persisted down to the present, old Korea was brought to an abrupt end in 1910 with the onset of the Japanese colonization of Korea, which lasted until the end of the Second World War in 1945.

Naturally the history of modern Korean poetry is short, for no substantial body of poems with modern sensibility and outlook appeared before the early part of the 20th century, when Korea started to awake from her long sleep of hermitage. Whereas traditional literature was primarily nurtured under the influence of Chinese literature, modern literature began to take shape with the impact of Western literary thought at the turn of the century. In other words, the early embryonic drive started with Practical Learning (1770s-1820s) by bringing Korea into direct contact with the West, ushering in the Era of Enlightenment, which extended roughly from 1880 to 1910.

Impelled by the surges of reform in political, educational, and social systems during the period, Korean literature was ready to embark on its modernization under the banner of New Style Literature, borne by Namsŏn Ch'oe in poetry and Kwangsu Yi in fiction. Ch'oe's "To the Boy from the Sea" came out in 1908 in his own magazine, *Sonyŏn* (The Boy), and Yi's early works in 1917. It must be pointed out in this context that, though these two figures are often mentioned as the fathers of modern Korean literature, they acted more as catalysts of modernizing Korean literature as a whole. More concerned with the didactic function of literature, they tended to employ art as a means of enlightening the people and enhancing social progress. To be more precise, Korean poetry started, in the historical perspective, with Yohan Chu and Ŏk Kim. Korean literature in general and Korean poetry in particular did not break out of its own shell of didacticism before the late 1910s, when the currents of 19th century European literary thought flowed into the literary world of Korea almost a century later.

Swayed neither by the influence of the sermonization of new style poems nor by the outburst of emotion of diluted romanticism, Chu and Kim succeeded in setting up a landmark with their lyrics written in the tradition of folk balladry. That is, it was with Chu and Kim that modern Korean poetry began to individualize itself. It seems advisable to note in passing that romanticism in Korea was not an exact copy of the western pattern. As in other areas of art, a comparison of Korean literature ought to be made in the context of Korean culture. It is true that poets looked into themselves to probe their own lives for sensation, like their counterparts in European countries, but the romantic notion of the unity of man and nature added an embittered spice of sorrow and melancholy to the

spirit of the times. Then, toward the mid-1920s, Chu and Kim were suc-
ceeded in turn by Tonghwan Kim and Sowŏl Kim. Unmistakably the best
poet of the period, Sowŏl Kim by far overshadowed Ŏk Kim, his teacher
and mentor, and distinguished himself by crystallizing the vernacular sen-
timents and pathos of the people in a string of gem-like poems such as
"The Azaleas," "Flowers in the Mountains," and "Invocation," to name a
few. He was the first to have a wide range of interest and a deep knowl-
edge of nature. He saw nature not merely as a center of beauty but also as
a source of intimations of life. By subtle manipulaton of paradox he made
things in nature vehicles for the expression of human situations. Contem-
porary with him, Tonghwan Kim, like Yŏngno Pyŏn and Tongmyŏng
Kim, reminisced on the beauty of the lost land. "When the River breaks
Loose" and "Snow Is Falling" are noteworthy pieces of the period. And
his "Frontier Night," though suffering from structural laxness, is the first
attempt made at a memorable epic poem. Nevertheless, the majority of
the lyric pieces written about this period were limited in scale and range,
and mainly concerned with sentiment. In the late 1920s, Sanghwa Yi and
Yong'un Han gave muscle to Korean poetry by incorporating into it the
texture of metaphysical depth and insight into human consciousness.
Despite his plunge into a romantic cave of sensuality and melancholy, Yi
was able to give articulate shape to his experience:

> Madonna, soon the day dawns, come over quickly
> before a temple bell mocks us.
> Let us go, your hands clinging around my neck, to
> the everlasting land in company with this night.
> (from "To My Bedroom")

Himself a devoted Buddhist monk as well as a patriot, Young'un Han
immortalized himself by turning out a series of poems. His *tour de force*
was evident in his collected poems, *The Silence of Love* (1925), which
embodies the metaphysical complexity and paradox of the human condi-
tion through Buddhistic formulas as well as poetic expression. According
to Buddhism, the self and the object are transmutable from the ontologi-
cal view point, as long as karma exists between the two, and with the loss
of the karma relationship, the self and the object perish at the same time.
The focal idea is illustrated in "I Do Not Know:"

> Burnt-out ashes turn to fuel again.
> Whose lamp is my heart that burns
> Flickering all night long?

When we think of history, we tend to think of a time-span character-
ized by certain events or consequence. It was in 1910 that Korea, after
nearly a decade of the loss of her identity as a nation, rose against Japanese

colonial rule. But the independent movement suffered defeat before the brutalities of the oppressors. The awakening national consciousness gathered momentum but the overwhelming sense of loss and despair soon plunged the nation again into darkness. In the midst of gloom, the prevailing sense of defeatism gave way to frustration and pessimism. Amid the vortex of decadence and confusion emerged a band of communist-oriented poets, who considered art merely as a means with which to fight the oppressors. Their works, however, hardly met the aesthetic standard of art. Way off from the chaos of the period, Sanghwa Yi found the articulate voices of the time in his, "Does Spring Come to the Forfeited Fields?":

> Does spring come to this land no more our own,
> to these forfeited fields?
> Bathed in the sun, I go as in a dream along a lane
> that cuts across paddy-fields like parted hair
> to where the blue sky and the green fields merge.

Toward the early 1930s the excessive heart-thumping and morbid sentimentalism ebbed away with the advent of intellectualism. At the same time the raving clamor of communist themes was on its way out in favor of art for art's sake. Yŏngnang Kim, Chiyŏng Chŏng and Sŏkchŏng Shin were among the finest poets of the period. Yongchŏl Park excelled more in theorizing about writing than in actual composition. Remembered for "The Departing Boat," Park enjoys a reputation more as a fine critic than a fine poet. Seriously concerned with the form and musicality of language, Yŏngnang Kim successfully created a dream-like atmosphere through the harmony of sense and sound. Chiyong Chŏng, on the other hand, carved image-reliefs in the modernistic tradition of the West. Sŏk-chŏng Shin, well remembered as the pastoral poet, spent the greater part of his boyhood in the remote countryside, where he developed into a conscientious craftsman, with a wide range of human interest and an intimate knowledge of country life. About this period, Kirim Kim made his appearance. Turning his back on the lyric tradition of poetry, he refused to follow his predecessors by seeking pure aesthetic ideals. Parnassian at heart, he introduced into Korean poetry a gallery of imagery devoid of the sentimental and the maudlin. His "The Weather Chart," in more than four hundred lines, reads in part:

> The channel
> is alive as sleek
> as the snakeback
> covered in
> bristling scales.
> Young mountain ranges are draped in colorful Arabian costumes

Kirim Kim was the first to get the reader acquainted with western poets like T. E. Hulme, Ezra Pound, W. H. Auden and T. S. Eliot. Kwangkyun Kim, who followed his example, wrote poems many of which surpassed Kirim Kim's. Written in the modernistic tradition, his "The Lyricism of an Autumn Day" and "Snowy Night" were considered the best pieces of the period. About this time, Sang Yi made his debut as a new poet. He showed disgust with the prevailing modes of expression and the conformist spirit of man by experimenting with surrealistic and Joycean stream-of-consciousness technique in his work. His "Flower-tree," for instance, can hardly make sense if handled on the surface of consciousness:

> In the midst of wilderness stands a flower tree,
> no other tree near it. It blossoms in passion as
> much as it yearns for its companion in some place.
> Yet it cannot call on its fellow tree it is so much
> in love with. I run away toward another tree
> as if I were the very flower tree.

In the late 1930s, poetry and literary magazines cropped up like the mushrooms after a rain. To this galaxy of poets belonged Ch'ŏnmyŏng No, Kwangsŏp Kim, Chŏngju Sŏ, Sŏkcho Shin and Ch'ihwan Yu. In revolt against the lifelessness and sand-dryness of modernist poems, Sŏ, for one, breathed vitality into Korean poetry. He sought for the life force through his magic wand of manipulating language, achieving some of the memorable pieces such as "The Snake" and "Midday." He gave through the mastery of his work the direction Korean poetry had to take. Yu was interested in seeking the essence on life and identity of his own being. Sangyong Kim, by contrast, felt happy on his retirement to the country-side. Other poets of this generation were Ch'ŏngmyŏng No and Yunsuk Mo. Perhaps in the long tradition of the regret and pain couched in po-ems by women, No's work concerned grief and bitterness of thwarted hope while Mo's projected a bright outlook on life. The 1930s witnessed before the close of the decade the three members of the Blue Deer Group, which links up with the lyric tradition of Korean poetry.Tujin Park, for instance, sought in nature the meaning of man's existence. Mogwŏl Park waved his magic rod over language to fashion rare gems, mostly in short poems. Lastly, Chihun Cho resorted to things past in rec-reating the beauty of the country. Again at this period Chŏngju Sŏ, now diverted from the Dionysiac life-fever, began to turn to pure lyricism in his "Beside the Chrysanthemum" and "The Nightingale." Ch'ihwan Yu sustained touch with the hard realities of the nation.

Thanks to the general panic during the war years, the 1950s saw few significant literary activities until well after the war ended. A rare exception was made in the case of the two poets, Tongju Yun and Yuksa Yi, both of whose poems were published after the war. Yi's "The Vertex" gave us a graphic picture of the dark times that tormented the nation:

> Gashed by the slashing of a harsh season
> I was driven at last to the north,
> where the bored heaven succumbed to the height
> and black frost cut my flesh.
> I do not know where to stretch my leg;
> where to land a single step.

In his "Wilderness" Yi found salvation only through his own sacrifice made for the good of his fellow men. The image of self-sacrifice is remarkably carved in "The Cross" by Tongju Yun:

> Should I have been allowed the cross
> as was Jesus Christ
> who suffered but was happy,
> I would gladly hang my own head
> and let my blood flow in quiet
> like a flower that blooms
> under the darkening skies.

At last "The Day" came that Hun Shim desparately and prophetically had wished for:

> When the day comes at last
> Mt. Samgak will leap in a joyful dance.
> When the day comes the waters of the Han
> will toss and roll in delight.
> If only the day comes before my life closes
> I will go and beat my head against the town bell
> to ring to the crows winging across the night sky.
> Even if my skull were crushed to pieces
> I would gladly die
> and I shall have no regrets.

The liberation period after the war saw a group of poets, among whom were Suyŏng Kim, Inhwan Park, Pyŏnghwa Cho, Tongjip Shin, Sang Ku, Hyŏnggi Yi and Tongju Yi. Most prolific of all, Cho vignetted the arabesque of city life and the loneliness of man. Suyŏng Kim emphasized the commitment of art to society, his work laced with suggestiveness and puns. Tongju Yi wove the tapestry of native Korean sentiment with the music of language.

The Korean War (1950-1953) virtually made a turning point in contemporary Korean poetry, within the framework of its long and diverse tradition. By and large, we can look at the post-war picture in three different frameworks. One is persistent in keeping to the agelong tradition. Among those who fit into this framework are Chaesam Park and Tongju Yi. Another group of poets has made a successful attempt at creating a new tradition with a strong dash of experientalism as well exemplified in "The Poppy" by Sŏngyong Park:

> Ready to faint when held;
> to crumble when hugged,
> that flower is no other than the opium
> poppy whose fume once drowsed
> the whole of China.
> Just a frail annual plant,
> it flares up my sunset garden
> with its charm and beauty.

Hijin Park adds to the vitality of the group. The third group likes to be identified with Suyŏng Kim, who defined the function of artists as serving for the betterment of human conditions, in a sense different from what the earlier propagandists pretended to claim. To this group belonged Tongyŏp Shin and Kyŏngnim Shin. Contemporary with them are a number of young poets like Tonggyu Hwang, Yŏngt'ae Kim, and Huran Kim, among others, who distinguished themselves during the 1960s. From the late 1960s to the mid-1970s quite a few new poets made their voices heard. With varied experiences and sensibilities, the new faces include Yŏjŏng Kim, Yangshik Kim, Un'gyŏ Kang, and Jaihiun Kim, who received an intensive training in creative writing in the United Sates before returning home to Korea to publish his poems in his native tongue. The three younger poets Sugwŏn Song, Hyŏngman Hŏ and Chŏnggwŏn Cho are on their own as distinctive voices. Lastly, highlighting his dogged resistance and protest against the establishment and his craving for the national reunification, Namju Kim represents many voices in the 1980s, following in the wake of Chiha Kim, Pong'u Park and Tongjip Shin before him.

Finally, I should like to thank all those poets who have allowd me to translate their works. Thanks are due to Larchwood Publication Ltd. to give me permission to use "Introduction" in this anthology.

1920s

Han, Yong'un (1879-1944)

Born in Hongsŏng, South Ch'ungchŏng, a devoted Buddhist monk since his early years, Han was one of the 33 members who in 1919 signed the historical document to declare Korea independent of the Japanese colonial rule. His poems concern his philosophical meditation on nature and the mystery of human existence. *The Silence of Love* (1926); *Complete Works of Han Yong-un* (1973).

THE SILENCE OF LOVE

Love is gone, gone is my love.
Tearing himself away from me he has gone
on a little path that stretches in the splendor of
a green hill into the autumn-tinted forest.
Our last oath, shining and enduring
like a gold-mosaicked flower,
has turned to cold ashes, blown away
in the breath of wind.
I remember his poignant first kiss and its memory
has wrought a complete change in my destiny,
then withdrawn into oblivion.
I hear not his sweet voice; I see not his fair looks.
Since it is human to love, I, alert, dreaded a
parting to come when we met.
The separation came so suddenly
it broke my heart with renewed sorrow.
Yet, I know parting can only destroy our love if
it causes futile tears to fall.
I would rather transfer the surge of this sorrow
onto the summit of hopefulness.
As we dread parting when we meet, so,
we promise to meet again when we part.
Though my love is gone, I am not parted from love;
an untiring love-song envelops the silence of love.

A SECRET IN EMBROIDERY

I have finished your clothes, a coat, gown,
and pajamas. All I have left to do is
embroidery on a pocket.
The pocket is thumb-stained because I've
fingered it many times before the finishing touch
yet to put.
Others may dismiss me as a poor worker,
but no one but me knows my secret.
When I feel sad and bitter and do embroidery
on the pocket, my mind passes through the needle-eye
after the gold thread, a bell-clear
song comes out of the pocket and becomes
my mind.
And, for all I know, there's no treasure
in the world worthy of the pocket.
This pocket I have not finished, not because
I feel reluctant, but because I wish it
really finished.

PARTING CREATES BEAUTY

Parting creates beauty.
There is no beauty of parting
in the ephemeral gold of the morning;
nor in the seamless black silk of the night;
nor in eternal life which admits no death;
nor in the gorgeous celestial flower that never fades.
O love, if there is no parting, I cannot come back
to life in laughter after tearful death.
O parting!
Parting creates beauty.

I DO NOT KNOW

Whose step is the paulownia leaf that falls silently
in vertical wavelets against the windless sky?

Whose looks are those patches of blue that peep
through the cracks in the dark clouds, driven
by the west wind after a long spell of rain?

Whose breath is this subtle scent that wafts
through the green moss on ancient trees,
no flower near,
to lure the quiet sky above an ancient pagoda?

Whose song is the little stream that flows,
God knows from where, tinkling over the pebbles?

Whose ode is the evening glow that graces the dying day
as it steps, lotus-flower soft, on the infinite seas
and touches the edgeless sky with its delicate hands?

The burnt-out ashes turn to earth again.
Whose lamp is my heart that burns all night long,
I know not for whom?

A SECRET

A secret? You mean a secret? What secret do I have?
I've tried to keep my secret from you but in vain.
My secret has entered your sight through my tears.
My secret has entered your hearing through my sighs.
My secret has entered your touch through my trembling heart.
One more secret, turned to a piece of red heart,
has entered your dream.
And the final secret cannot be expressed in so many words,
like a voiceless echo.

THE ESSENCE OF LOVE

To call love by name is no longer love.
What words or phrases can properly describe it?
How can the smiling rose-lips in agony ever
touch it?
How can the eyes of autumnal waters, reflecting
the dark side of sorrow behind tears,
ever see through it?
Love is an entity beyond the shadowless clouds,
beyond the echoless cliffs, and beyond the
unpassable sea of the mind.
Love's essence cannot be felt in your mind nor
in your eyes.
Love's secret lies only in the needle that has
embroidered your handkerchief, in the flowers
you have planted, in your very sleep, and
in the imagination of poets.

THE FERRYBOAT AND THE TRAVELER

I am a ferry boat. A traveler, you tread on me
with muddy shoes. I take you aboard to cross
the river. With you held in my arms, I go across
the currents, deep, shallow, or rapid.
If you do not turn up, I await you from dawn
to dusk, despite the wind, rain, or snow.
Yet, once you've crossed the river, you do not
look back on me. But I believe you will be coming
back some day.
I grow old and worn-out waiting for you
day after day.
I am a ferryboat. You are a traveler.

Kim, Ŏk (1893-195?)

Born in Kwaksan, North Pyong'an Province, Kim was kidnapped to North Korea during the Korean War (1950). Educated both in Korea and Japan, he worked as a teacher, a reporter and a writer for a radio broadcasting station. Kim started his literary career in 1918 when he introduced into *The Western Literature Bulletin,* a weekly, a number of leading 19th century poets such as P. Verlaine, C. Baudelaire and R. Gourmont. In 1919 he became one of the initial members of *The Creation,* a pure literary magazine. *Dance of Anguish* is known to be the first collection of translated works from western literature ever published in Korea. Kim's poetry is a lament for the transiency and insignificance of human existence. As a major influence on Kim Sowŏl, Kim Ŏk considered rhyme scheme to be an integral part of his poetic architecture. His work includes *A Song of Jellyfish* (1923), *A Song of Spring* (1925), *The Golden Sands* (1925), *Collected Poems of Kim Ŏk* (1929), *When Dawn Breaks* (1947) and many others including translations.

A SPINNING WHEEL

A spinning wheel
Wheels in a moan.
Yesterday and today alike
I wheel in joy;
Man's life wheels in cares.

A spinning wheel
Wheels in a moan.
Threads reel off a tangled skein;
Dreamy world gets more tangled.

A spinning wheel
Wheels in a moan.
Now my prince would wind threads on a reel
And then cry in my arms over his tangled skein.

A spinning wheel
Wheels in a moan.
Let my prince's tangled skein be disentangled.
O how can I undo his tangled skein?

SAMSU-KAPSAN*

Would that I returned to Samsu-kapsan.
Where can Samsu-kapsan be, I wonder?
Over peaks folded in peaks fleecy clouds herd.

Would that I saw Samsu-kapsan.
How far off is it, I wonder?
What could be more rugged than this path?

Where can Samsu-kapsan be, I wonder?
I cannot return to Samsu-kapsan.
If only I were a bird to fly over the distance!

Would that I returned to Samsu-kapsan.
Would that I saw Samsu-kapsan.
O cruelty! Only my dreams come and go.

* Kim Sowŏl wrote his "Samsu-kapsan" on the model of his mentor's poem.

A SEAGULL

Over the waves leaping and laughing
Intoxicated with spring perfume
A sea gull wanders, white.

When the sinking sun begins
To remove its lingering glory
A sea gull streaks white
Across the darkening sea.

Over the evening sea that
Retires calmly in ripples
Golden dreams of my childhood
Fade lonely like a sea gull
Wandering, white.

WINTER

Limbs jerking upright,
Tree is moaning in a shiver,
Complaining of a cruel wind
That slashes its naked body.

In pity of the shivering tree
The heaven makes a white downy bed
And soothes it into sleep.

The tree sleeps under the snow-quilt
Hugging its hope for tomorrow,
Weeping at heart over the harsh season.

Never tell me life can be whipped to death.
All comes back to life again in spring.

SPRING BREEZE

Gently and softly
It dances with leaves.

Softly as feathers
It kisses the flowers.

Wavering gossamer-like
It has gone nowhere.

The gentle breeze
Is my soul sorely sick for love.

O, Sangsun (1894-1963)

Born in Seoul, better known by his pen name Kong-ch'o, he studied Buddhistic philosophy at Tojisha University in Japan. As a bohemian he wandered across the country to visit temples for meditation. He was affiliated with *The Ruins* group (1920). Despairing of the national situation after the defeat of the Independence Movement, he gave himself up for a while to nihilistic abandon. He was also a great chain-smoker, known to have consumed 200 cigarettes a day.

THE FIRST NIGHT

Now night is far advanced.
The candle is out for the bridal night,
Garments of vanity shedding.

Bare bodies of youth
Swim like fish
In the sea of darkness.
Suddenly
A faint cry cuts the air:
Oh! . . . hurt me.

Sound that cracks open the secret
Of life in the beginning.
Sound that leads one life
To eternal life.
Sound that opens the gate of nirvana.
O everlasting St. Mary!

The countless stars
In the faraway skies
Shine in splendor for the night.

The night pregnant with dawn
Advances into the pitch-dark deep.

POETRY, CIGARETTES AND I

Poetry, cigarettes and I
Are a trinity of identical tune with differing tones,

Seized by poetic spirit I
Keep spewing volumes of smoke

Which flees on the wing of curved melody
into the infinite blue of skies.

WANDERLUST

1
How my soul
Swings
On the endless flow;
swings
on the endless flow!

Sick for the sea
Where there is no sea
I fetch the sea
Into my mind, eyes closed,
Sitting quietly
Forgetful of ticking time.

Tiptoeing on the cold castle-top
I watch the far-off sea
Barely visible beyond the hills and ridges
Forgetful of the flush of sunset.

When I gaze on the sea
Rolling in the mind
The deep sound of the sea
Sobs in my blood vessels.

The endless savannah of the sea
Opens onto my mind's eye;
The mist-like scent of the sea
Lingers in my nose.

2

Traveler's soul;
O traveler's soul
Wandering everlastingly.
My soul swings on the breast of wandering.

I weep
To see the world where nothing lacks.
I weep
To see the world which lacks all.
I weep
To see the infinite world.
I weep
To see the finite world
I weep
To see the world where being and non-being alternate.
I weep
When I land where my feet of flesh touch.
I weep
To see the world where life and death crisscross.
I weep
When I land where my feet of soul slips into the bottomless
world.

I weep, bottomless and fathomless.
I weep.

Hwang, Sŏg'u (1895-1958)

Born in Seoul, Hwang studied political science and economics at Waseda University in Japan. A reporter before the war and a college professor after the war, Hwang once identified himself with anarchists. His poems were published in *The Ruins* in the '20's. He started *The Rose Village*, the first coterie magazine in Korea (1921). Like Kim,Ŏk and Chu, Yohan, he came under the influence of symbolism, especially in his earlier works. His book of poems *A Song of Nature* came out in 1928.

THE HEART OF A GIRL

The heart of a girl is a spring lawn:
If trodden, it breaks;
If kindled, it burns.

The heart of a girl is a glass-bell:
If wind brushes, it sobs;
If tossed, it shatters.

MOUNTAIN FLOWERS IN THE DUSK

Like a girl
In the mountain inn
Soliciting wayfarers for the night
The bell-flowers
Handsomely decorating
The vales and the bases
Hold on to the wind
And bow suggestively
To every passer-by.

A BUTTERFLY HAS FLOWN AWAY

Into the yellow canna
About to unfold its petals
A white butterfly has flown
With a secret design.

A white butterfly has flown
With a secret design
Into the yellow canna
Unoccupied as a house
Except by a lonely girl.

SPRING

Autumn gone, spring is freed from bondage.
The breeze softly plays on a flute in the trees.
I wind thread on a spool and tie it to the flower-bed
And pull the breezes one after another.

Autumn gone, spring breaks free from bondage.
Between us two, in the shade of heart,
The string sound rings.
O birds, peaks, gentle rain and moon!

FALLEN LEAVES

Fallen leaves,
a shedding of bodily laving
of trees and plants
after childbirth.

Fallen leaves
are words, writ large
on the ground, recording
in autobiography their joyful labor.

Pyŏn, Yŏngno (1898-1961)

Born in Seoul, graduated from San Jose College, U.S., Pyŏn taught at Ewha Womens University, at Sŏng-kyunkwan University and at Naval Academy of Korea. Later, he worked with newspapers. In the initial stage of modern Korean poetry, Pyŏn made himself conspicuous by his brilliant wit and rhetoric. He was awarded the 1st Cultural Prize (1948). His work includes *The Korean Mind* (1924) and *The Azaleas*, a book of poems in English (1947).

NON'GE*

Her holy anger was
Deeper than a religious faith;
Her burning passion,
Stronger than love.

On the waves
Bluer than blue bean-flowers
Her heart flowed in ripples
Redder than red poppies.

Her charming eyebrows
Poised aloft in grace;
Her pomegranate lips
Kissed death.

On the waves
Bluer than blue bean-flowers
Her heart flowed in ripples
Redder than red poppies.

The rippling waves
Will flow eternally blue;
Her fair soul
Will be blazing eternally red.

* A legendary *kisaeng*, patriotism incarnate. She was invited to the victory celebration of a group of Japanese generals who had led their invading armies into Korea in the 16th century. When the party reached its height she embraced one of the generals to throw herself with him off a cliff into the river.

On the waves
Bluer than blue bean-flowers
Her heart flows in ripples
Redder than red poppies.

THE MIND OF KOREA

Where is the mind of Korea to be sought?
Where is it to be sought?
Shall we look into the cave?
Shall we dredge up the bottom of the sea?
Shall we clear the thickset branches of willows?
Or shall we look for heaven's rim far off?
Where is the mind of Korea to be sought?
The mind of Korea has lost its direction.
Sad.

I TRADE MY DREAMS

I have tried to trade my dreams for solitude
And live in the mountain deep,
But birds of all kinds come to sing in your voice,
And flowers of all kinds smile reminding me of you.
I have tried to trade my dreams for solitude
And grow old quietly by the sea,
But myriad waves kick up my heels
And the sky, the far-off sails and the sands
Conspire to call back every bit of memory.
Born between dreams and solitude
We perish between solitude and dreams.
I must go calm and quiet
Like stars studded in the sky,
Like the moon moored in the empty sky.

SPRING RAIN

A voice is calling, low and quiet.
I go out, yes, I go out to see
A drowsy milky cloud drift
As if in a hurry yet leisurely enough
Across the azure sky.
Oh! I miss something that I have not lost.

A voice is calling, low and quiet,
I go out, yes, I go out to see
A breath of flowers float,
Like dim memories of the past,
Trembling and invisible luxuriating in its own scent
My heart aches, unhurt.

A voice calling, low and quiet.
I go out, yes, I go out only to see
No trace of milky cloud or flower-breath
But silver threads of spring rain
Falling quietly like a brooding thought,
Fit to wet a pigeon's pink feet.
How I expect someone who will not come!

Chu, Yohan (1900-1979)

Born in Pyŏng'yang in North Korea, educated both in China and Japan, Chu spearheaded the rank of New Poetry in breaking with traditional poetry. He was editor of *The Creation*, the first literary magazine in Korea. Despite the prevailing sense of frustration after the Samil Independence Movement, Chu's poems were bright and hopeful in tone. As he confessed in the preface to his *Beautiful Dawn*, he consciously kept himself from falling into the decadent mood of the times. His work includes *Beautiful Dawn* (1924), *Peach Blossoms* (1930), "Fireworks," a prose poem (1919), and *Poems by Three Poets* (1929).

THE SOUND OF RAIN

It is raining.
Night quietly unfolds her feathers;
Rain whispers in the yard like chickens
Peeping among themselves.

The moon going thread-thin,
Warm breezes start to rise as if
The spring trickles down from the stars.
Rain is falling this dark night.

Rain is raining
Gently like a kind guest calling.
I open the window to greet him;
Rain is raining, quiet and invisible.

It is raining in the yard,
Outside the window, on the roof.
Rain is raining to fetch glad tidings
For my private joy.

FIREWORKS

The day is drawing in. The evening-glow sinks in the lonely river, crimsoning the western sky. With sunset comes another night when I must cry my heart out in the shade of an apricot tree. Today is Buddha's birthday, the eighth of the fourth month, and crowds of people throng about in the streets, all in a festive mood. But why should I be left alone in sorrow amid stir and bustle of the celebration?

So many balls of fire are madly dancing. As I watch them from the fortress gate of the town, the smell of water and sandy flats assails my nostrils, fulgent torches swaying and scraping the sky. And then unsatisfied, they go on consuming themselves. A young man, with darkness cutting into his heart, tries to toss his purple dreams of the past into the waters of the river. Can the heartless flow of the river stop his thin shadow? How flowers can stand fresh when plucked off? As good as dead in life, lost in the thought of my beloved, shall I let this flame burn out my heart, burn down my sorrow? Just yesterday I dragged my lead-heavy feet to the grave-yards and found flower-buds unfolding from where they had been lying dead in the winter. But how about love's spring? Will it never come back? I would rather put an end to all, by plunging into the water. Yet, who will ever pity me, lament over my loss? Suddenly, crack, crack, shoots up a rocket fire, a shower of sparks spread fanwise. I come to. The explosive laughter of the spectators sounds as if to mock and accuse me. Would that I lived a more passionate life, a flaming life, like those fireworks leaping up their tongues from smouldering smoke, even in their burning agony. My burning heart craves for something to match it.

When the warm April breeze strokes across the river, the crowds dressed white start to mill about on Moran Hill by the clear water. And at a gentle touch of wind, the firy wavelets laugh a lunatic laugh and the fish dart scared into the sand-bed for shelter. Aboard the boat floating on the currents, figures of men rock to the drowsy dancing rhythms, shadows flickering in a peal of laughter, and then a youthful courtesan sings in a drawn-out voice under a lantern hanging overhead. Now the blazing fireworks subsided, cup after cup of wine wears me out. I lie stretched on the filthy bottom of the boat, idle tears soaking my cheeks. Sick of the incessant dinning of the drum, some dash out of the boat, their eyes flashing with refueled desire, the candlelight guttering drowsily on the rumpled skirt-folds.

And the oarlocks alone squeak as if to give some meaning; they weigh down my heart.

Look how the river laughs! A sinister laugh. The chill water laughs looking up to the blackening sky. The boat comes into view, gliding down the waves, oarlocks squeaking, accompanied by sorrow by every gusty wind.

Row your boat against the rapid currents of the Taedong river all the way down to the Nŭng-na Isle, where your sweetheart awaits standing barefoot on the bank. Head straight where she is. What of the chill gust rising in the wake of the boat? What of the sinister laughter? What of the dark and depressed heart of a love-lorn youth? Light follows shadow. Seize the day. That is the only certainty. Boy, live today, enjoying tonight, enjoy your own red-flaming torch, your red-lips, your eyes and your red tears.

A GUEST

Outside the window
Someone has come for me.
In the room fatigue
Prompts my eyes to be shuttered.
I look out through a window chink;
Nothing is there but wind and night.

Outside the window
Someone has come for me.
I hesitate to open
The window.
'If' gives me causeless fears.
Shall I see him in the morning?

Outside the window
Someone has come for me.
My whole frame seems to burst
With 'expectancy'.
I rise, resolved, and open the window;
The moonlight long in waiting
Baptizes my naked body.

I WISH TO SING

Like a fish breathing in fresh water;
Like a lark soaring into the blue sky;
Like a boat setting sail before the wind;
I wish to sing so freely.

Like the sunshine spangling on the white sands;
Like waves breaking against the bank;
Like a child playing with ripples on the beach;
I wish to sing so listlessly.

Yi, Sanghwa (1900-1941)

Born in Taegu, North Kyŏngsang Province, Yi studied French at Tokyo University of Foreign Studies, Japan. Affiliated with *The White Waves* circle, Yi wrote in his early years romantic poems with a touch of sentimentality. Later, Yi succeeded in crystallizing the misery of the oppressed nation into "Does Spring Come to These Forfeited Fields?" Yi's poems were posthumously collected by Paek Ki-man in *Sang-hwa And Kowol* (1951).

DOES SPRING COME TO THESE FORFEITED FIELDS?

Does spring come to this land no more our own,
to these forfeited fields?
Bathed in the sun I go as if in a dream along a lane
that cuts across paddy-fields like parted hair
to where the blue sky and the green field meet.
You mute heaven and silent fields,
I do not feel I have come here on my own;
tell me if I am driven by you or by some hidden force.

The breeze that whispers in my ears
strokes my garment at every step;
the larks behind the clouds are caroling
like maidens across the fence.
You rich green fields of corn,
have you washed the cataracts of your hair
in that gentle rain that fell last night?
I feel so refreshed and light in the head.

Alone as I am, my steps are cheerful
for the kind water in the ditch
rushes past the thirsty fields
with rippling songs of lullaby.
Swallows and butterflies, be gentle and modest.
I must say hello to the cocks-comb-flowering village.
How I wish to have another look at those fields,
weeded by women, their hair oil-shining.

Hand me a hoe that I may work in an honest sweat;
that I may walk on this earth soft as rich breasts
till my ankles grow numb with pain.
My soul yearns for the infinite as that of children
frolicking on the riverbank.
Tell me what it is you are craving for,
whither you go.
Soaked in the smell of the greening earth
I walk all day long limping between the green of sorrow
and joy as if possessed by the spirit of spring.

But now that the land is no more our own
spring can no longer be our own.

PARTING

Must we part? Must we, you and I?
We loved in secret not knowing we would part,
we would part in secret.

My heart and lips tremble in the height of passion.
I cannot even breathe, much less can I speak.
How can I be blind to your heartache
when our two lives are about to go dreamy tonight?

Love, watch the sky overcast;
watch the earth about to sink.
Love, do I look alive as yesterday?
Are you alive sitting beside me?

Must we part? Must we, you and I?
Let us be the stars so that we can see each other
rather than live apart and think apart.

Is love a mere laughing, frail reed
on the drifting mind?
Does a flower glory in season
and then fall to decay out of season?

Did you find faith only in waiting for your love?
Did you find loneliness in the hate of your love?
Why did I hate to suffer,
blind to mockery when seeking happiness?

Love, black shadow hovers over our minds
where there's no boundary drawn
as in water mixed with water.

We loved in secret without knowing
we would part in secret.
Let us be nightingales and weep in bleeding
tears rather than live apart as humans.

Come and hold me tight against your body;
I want to have our two hearts welded into one.
Let us give ourselves free to abandon,
our eyes closed in mutual shyness and faith.

Are the lines on your face caused by the parting pain?
Come to me, driving parting away.
Run into my arms ready to clasp
your ivory-cross waist.

Love, give me your hand; place in mine
your wax-colored hand visible in the dark.
Love, speak to me, to my eyes, the silent
words fit for the dumb.

Must we part? Must we, you and I?
Shall we drown into the sea and be a merman
and a mermaid rather than live apart in madness?

TO MY BEDROOM

Madonna, night is returning weary of feast.
Come to me before dawn with dew glinting
on your peach breasts.

Madonna, come to me only in body, shedding all
the pearls enjoyed visually for ages.
Let us hurry, for we are the two stars that must hide when the
day dawns.

Madonna, I am waiting for you shivering with fear
in the dark and deserted street of my mind.
Oh, how soon cocks crow, dogs bark!
My lady, do you hear too?

Madonna, let us go to my bedroom that I have
adorned all night for you.
The old moon is sinking; I hear footfalls—Oh,
are they yours?

Madonna, look how mind's candlelight quietly
bemoans with its wick burning low.
It may be blown out any minute, choked in a whiff of wind.

Madonna, mountain shadow way over is approaching
mute as a ghost.
My heart pounds wildly lest someone may see us.
My lady, I call you.

Madonna, soon the day dawns. Come over on a run
before the temple bell mocks us.
Let us go, your arms tight around my neck,
to the everlasting land in company with the night.

Madonna, no one will enter my bedroom
across the one-log-bridge of regret and dread.
Oh, the wind is arising. Come lightly as the wind.
Are you coming, my lady?

Madonna, what a pity! Am I mad that I hear a sound
that doesn't sound?
My soul and body are burning, as if my whole blood,
my whole inner spring has gone dry.

Madonna, we must go sooner or later.
Why don't we go then at our own free will,
unforced?

You are my *Maria* who believes me, because
you know my bedroom is a cave of resurrection.
Madonna, there is no difference: the dreams that
night brings us, the dreams we spin and the dreams
of life that enwrap us.
So let us go to my bedroom, which is timeless
as a boy's heart.

Madonna, the star's laughing is dying away;
the dark night's waves are subsiding.
Oh, come to me before the fog breaks away.
I call you, my lady.

Chŏng, Chiyong (1901-195 ?)

Born in Okchŏn, North Ch'ungchŏng Province, Chŏng studied English literature at Tojisha University, Japan. During World War II he taught at high schools and after the war was Professor at Ehwa Women's University. He was forced into North Korea during the Korean War (1950-1953). One of the most influential poets during the twenties, Chŏng brought vigor and modernistic images dashed with vernacular sentiments into Korean poetry. His books are *Collected Poems* (1935), *Paeknok Tarn* (1941) and *Selected Poems* (1946).

NATIVE VILLAGE

When I come back home, to my native village
I find it not as sweet as it used to be.

The pheasants brood as before in the mountains
and cuckoos sing their seasonal carols.

But my heart is homeless, belonging nowhere
and drifts as a cloud over a far-away port.

Again today as I alone go up a hilltop
a flower smiles sweetly, my lips gone dry and bitter.

When I come back home, to my native village
the blue expanse of sky spreads high and endless.

THE SUMMIT

Cliffs are tinged red
as with cinnabar.
The waters flower dew-clear.
Poised on a perilous perch of a tree
a red-winged bird pecks at fruit.
Wild grape-vines have budded green.
A scented snake lies coiled up in plateau-dreams.
The summit of height towers, majestic like death,
where birds of passage first visit;
the crescent moon sinks
and a double rainbow begins to form.
A view from below makes it look as high as Orion.
I step onto the topmost crag
a white flower the size of a star waves.
I brace my feet, my legs dandelion-stalk thin.
The east sea where the sun rises
seems to beat against my cheeks
like a flap flapping in the breeze.

NOSTALGIA

Winding eastward through a wide plain
the brook murmured an old tale on its way;
a brindle ox lowed lazily
in the golden glow of sunset.
How can I ever forget that place even in dreams?

When fire was going out in an earthen brazier,
the wind galloped across the desert plain;
resting his head on a straw-roll
my old father would take a nap.
How can I ever forget that place even in dreams?

Brought up with soil, my heart was aglow
with longing for the bright blue sky;
Once I shot an arrow at random into the air
and got soaked while searching the wet bushes.
How can I ever forget that place even in dreams.

My sister would wear her raven hair long
like night waves in a legendary sea;
my simple-hearted wife led a plain life,
dispensing with foot-wear for all seasons.
They would often glean a field with the sun on their backs.
How can I ever forget that place even in dreams?

Under the skies studded sparsely with stars,
I would go for a secret sand-castle;
autumn crows cawed winging over a thatched hut
where I would join my friends and chat around a dim-lit lamp.
How can I ever forget that place even in dreams?

THE GLASS-WINDOW

Something sad and chill glimmers on the glass.
Fervorless, it sticks to the breath-clouded surface,
flapping its frozen wings as if out of habit.
I wipe it clean trying to see through it.
Only the black night rolls out and in against the glass.
And the watered stars twinkle, studded like jewels.
Every night I wipe the glass all alone,
driven by my lonely entranced heart,
my lovely blood vessels burst in the lungs.
O my son, you've fled like a mountain-bird.

Yi, Changhŭi (1900-1929)

Born in Taegu, North Kyŏngsang Province, Yi committed suicide at the age of 26. When Yi appeared on the literary scene in 1925 through *The Korean Literary World*, the literary world was swayed by sentimentalism and the decadent mood of the times. Yi, however, was not affected by the morbid spirit. He held his own ground. His poems were fresh and sensuous like those by modernists. *Sanghwa-And Kowŏl* (Yi's pen name), a posthumous collction of two poets, was published in 1951.

SPRING IS A CAT

The cat's coat, soft as pollen,
distills a scent of sweet spring.

In the cat's eyes round as golden bells
Dances a flame of mad spring.

On the cat's lips, quiet and closed,
Plays a drowsiness of mild spring.

On the sharp whiskers of the cat
Leaps the sparkling life of green spring.

A LONESOME SEASON

Autumn is well on its way;
Fields and hills and forests
Look seared and grey.

High on the hilltop
A dog howls
into the air.

In the empty plain
Burning leaves raise
thin smoke.

My dear,
Now is time for us
To meditate in piety.

THE INSECT CRIES

The insect chirring every night
Chirrs again today under the floor.

Like a stream silvering at evening
The insect chirrs, cold and lonesome.

My heart is drawn to the insect
chirring nightly under the floor.

Kim, Tonghwan (1901-19 ??)

Born in Kyŏngsŏng, North Hamgyŏng Province, Kim was taken by force into the north during the Korean War (1950). He studied at Toyo University in Japan. He began his literary career with *Frontier Night*, the first epic poem ever written in Korea. His works embrace nationalistic ideals. He was editor of *Three Thousand Li*, a literary magazine. His work includes *Frontier Night* (1924), *Soaring Youth* (1925), *A Sweet Briar* (1942) and *A Wing Returned* (1962).

WHEN THE RIVER BREAKS LOOSE

When the river breaks loose
A boat will come;
Aboard her will come
My sweet love.

If my love comes not
Her message will come aboard the boat.
Again today I wait by the riverside
And return home, empty-hearted.

If my love comes
This grief in me will melt away
As river stark-frozen in midwinter
Breaks loose in good time.

The river will break loose in no time.
What keeps it from melting, I wonder?
Again today I wait by the riverside
And return home, empty-hearted.

IN THE SOUTH VILLAGE ACROSS THE HILL

1

Who ever lives in the south village across the hill
That the spring breeze is blowing southward?

When it is flowering time of April the azaleas perfume the air.
When wheat ripens in May the wheat scent fills the air.

Can't I have any of them wind-borne for me?
What a joy when the south wind blows in the south village!

2

Who ever lives in the south village across the hill
That the sky spreads in such a beautiful color?

Over the expanse of green grass monarchs hover in groups.
Over the brook bickering down the willows the larks sing.

I climb up the ridge driven by a longing
Can't I have any of them wind-borne for me?
What a joy when the south wind blows in the south village?

3

In the south village across the hill stands a pear-tree.
Who can it be that stands under the tree?

I climb up the ridge driven by a longing
Nothing is visible screened by the clouds.

The faint notes of the song ringing on and off
Come to me in the waves of the wind.

SNOWFALL

In the north snow falls for days and nights on end.
When the swirling snow thickens in the grey sky
I see the northern tip of my land loom in the snow.

Once in a while a donkey brays in the snow-storm
That has sucked sands from the northern shore
To whiplash us exiles into freezing cold.

So cold, no guest from afar can stay for the night.
We must send those back home on a sledge
Who call us in spring to see flowering forsythias.

When polar bears growl, Ursa Major twinkling,
We hug each other to dance on the ice-coated wild
Pointing to the red star, longing for the clime
Of swallow and glancing at foreigners,
Their eyes sparkling blue lit by the fire.

In the cold of the north, in the numbing cold of the night
A smuggling wagon rattles across the frozen river
Its tinkling bell muffled by the cracking of ice.

Snow is falling white, piling cream-white
On the loaded removal van heading northward.
Snow falls quietly in thickening fleece.

WHEN SPRING COMES

When spring comes azaleas bloom in the hills and fields.
Where the azaleas bloom, my heart also blooms.
When the maidens from the next village come to pick the
flowers,
Let them pick my own heart with the flowers.

When spring comes larks start their songs in the sky.
Where the larks sing my own song is also sung.
When the maidens come to gather wild greens,
Let them hear my own song with the lilting larks.

When spring comes I miss you so.
Let me be a lark and send you my message.
When spring comes I miss you so.
Let me be an azalea and smile.

THE BOATSONG OF THE SUNGARI

Clouds scud in patches on the dawning skies.
Yo-heave-ho, yo-heave-ho, let us move on.
Where clouds sail
my heart also sails.

We've left our homeland a thousand *li* * behind.
Yo-heave-ho, yo heave-ho, let us move on.
We've come a thousand *li* so far;
We have a thousand *li* to go yet.
We've left our homeland
With love tied to it.

Yo-heave-ho, yo-heave-ho, let us move on.
Even the waters of the Sungari moan.
Yo-heave-ho, yo-heave-ho, let us move on.
Is the river alone weeping?
We are weeping, too.

* 16 *li* equals a mile.

Kim, Tongmyŏng (1901-1966)

Born in Kangnŭng, Kangwŏn Province, Kim majored in theology at Aoyama Academy in Japan. His career ranged widely from a teacher at all levels of school to a newspaper editorial writer and Congressman. During the Japanese colonial rule he made his home in the countryside, where he wrote poems with nostalgia for his lost homeland. After the Korean War he found his theme in the immediate realities. His work includes *My Lyre* (1930); *Plantain* (1938), *The Witness* (1955), and *My Heart* (1964).

MY HEART

My heart is a lake:
Come and row your boat on it.
I will embrace your white shadow and
Break into so many jewels against your sides.

My heart is a candle-light:
Please close the window for me.
I will burn myself quietly to the last drop,
Trembling by your silken dress.

My heart is a traveler:
Play on your flute for me.
I will stay the whole night through
Listening to your tunes under the moon.

My heart is a falling leaf:
Let me stay in your garden awhile.
I will leave you like a lonely wanderer
When the wind rises again.

AUTUMN

Your heart is a deserted sandbar;
Passion has receded like a lake
And the sad gravestone of an
Unfinished tale remains.

Is dream a fallen leaf?
Red blood on the sleeves
Remains unwashed,
Inveterate rancor.

Your touch is so cold, I know why.
Now please place your hand on my forehead.
O my lady! You are sad and beautiful
Like a young widow.

THE SEA

I restore my youth
Only when her rich dress
Drapes my feet.

When I feel at last her massive
Arms around my waist,
I fall into a trance where my bones
Gleam, shell-like, in her bosom.

If my bosom could be a little port
The swelling waves would be the sea-farers
Who bring exotic dreams from afar;
My heart rises and falls like weeds.

A BANANA PLANT

How long since you left your homeland?
What a pitiful dream you must dream!

Burning sick for home in the south
Your soul seems lonelier than a nun's.

You are a passionate woman athirst for a shower;
I draw water from the well to shower your feet.

Night is chill now and
I will let you stay near my bed.

I will be your willing servant
Sheltered from winter in your warm silken skirt.

Kim, Sowŏl (1902-1934)

Better known by his pen name, Kim Chŏngsik was born in Kwaksan, North Pyŏng'an Province and died in 1934. As early as 1920 when he was 17, his genius manifested itself in a series of poems such as "Flowers in the Hill," "A Spring Wanderer," and others which appeared in *The Beginning* (Kaebyok or Creation). Those were followed by another string of lyrical jewels including "The Azaleas" in 1922. Practially all of his work, about 250 pieces known so far, were written in a period of 5 years in and after 1920. He is unmistakably one of the greatest poets ever born in Korea. His collected poems *Azaleas* came out in 1925.

THE AZALEAS

If you go away
because you cannot bear with me
in silence I bid you Godspeed.

Azaleas aflame on Yaksan Hill*
I will gather with full hands
and scatter them in your path.

Tread with a tread,
light and gentle,
on the flowers as you go.

If you go away
because you cannot bear with me
no tears will I weep though I perish.

* A scenic spot noted for azaleas in the far north of Korea.

FLOWERS IN THE HILLS

Flowers bloom
in the hills;
Spring, summer and autumn through
Flowers bloom.

In the hills
Far and near
Flowers bloom;
Way up in solitude.

Little birds that carol
in the hills.
They live in the hills
For the love of flowers.

Flowers fade
in the hills;
Spring, summer and autumn through
Flowers fade.

THE GRAVES

A voice is calling me, calling.
The rows of gravestones here and there
Sway in the moon, dotting the reddish mounds.
My tuneless song, a mere sound, condenses into grief,
Ancestral records are buried here;
I must search them all over the place.
My song, tuneless, spreads
Over the mounds lying dappled in shadows.
A voice is calling me, calling,
Calling me, calling.
It calls me drawing my soul toward it.

LOVE-PILLOW

Shall I gnash my teeth
And die?
The moon sprinkles its beam
On the window.

Lying huddled in tears
I pillow my head on my arm.
A spring pheasant cries,
Sleepless, in the night.

Where has gone now
The love-pillow
That we once shared
In an eternal vow of burning love?

In the spring hill
Far and near
Cuckoos carol,
Calling their mates.

Where has gone now
The love-pillow?
The moon sprinkles its beam
On the window.

UNFORGETTABLE

You'll miss me and remember me.
Life is such; take it as it comes
and some day you will forget.

You'll miss me and remember me.
Let years roll by the way they go
and you will forget more or less.

Then you may protest:
How could I ever forget
when tenderness tears me apart?

INVOCATION

O name shattered to pieces!
O name vanished into the void!
O name without response!
I will be calling it to my death.

O my love,
You are gone before I have said
What I have carved for you in my heart.
While in the west a glory burns the blue
Even a herd of deer weeps mournfully.
Your name I call standing on a lone hill.

I call you till sorrow chokes me.
I call till sorrow chokes me.
But my voice vainly echoes in the vast void
unable to reach you.

Though I turn to stone
I will be calling your name.
O my love, my love.

SONG BY THE BROOK

Were you born a wind
you might brush my lapels in the empty
plain where a brook runs moonbeamed.

Were you born a slug
we might dream together, though idle,
on a mountain pass in the rainy night.

Were you born a stone
on the cliffs washed by the waves
I would hug you to roll into the sea below.

Were I a flame-spirit
I could burn your heart all night
till both of us turn to ashes.

1930s

O, Ilto (1901-1946)

Born in Yŏng'yang, North Kyongsang Province, O (his real name being Hibyŏng) studied philosophy at Rikkyo University in Japan. His poems came out in the early 30's. He was editor of *The Poetry Garden* (1934-1935). As a recurring theme of his poems, desolation of human spirit and malady of the times made for creating the beauty of lyricism.

FIRESIDE ELEGY

The wind blowing hard the night through
Must have shaken the persimmon tree in the back
Hill down to its last leaf.

The season that falls—every single leaf,
A drop of hot crimson blood will be listlessly
Trampled by village children.

O my broken bell incapable of appointment,
Must you ever watch the lonesome night sky?
A sharp scream of wild geese winging heavenward
Dies over the green land, land of heart's desire.

I close my eyes now by the quiet fireside;
Nostalgia's misty rain blurs my sight.

The dream-like days of old, O my love.
How long have I been exiled from your warm breast?

Despite storms and the boundless desert
I have come out of breath, my heart torn off.

Why should I leave it rusty,
The cold steel sheathed in my heart?

Over the cold mute ashes come and go
Armies of confusing thoughts.

White snow will soon fall in heavy flakes
On the hills and fields;
The sun will go down.

MY SWEETHEART, COME CLOSER

My sweetheart, come closer.
Grief-stricken, autumn is far advanced.

From over the ruined castle in the black night
The north wind blows soughing over us.

In a blouse thin as butterfly wings.
How chilling! How you shiver! How frightening!

My sweetheart, come closer.
Now is time to fall; time waits not for us.

The leaves once gloried in summer splendor.
Now fall, sobbing under the castle wall.

Life is like leaves blown in the wind.
Where shall we meet once blown apart?

Come closer to me.
Though within a step's distance, I feel myself
A world apart from you.

All my blood surges into my heart.
I may burn myself down before dawn breaks.
What thought dwells in your black eyes?

Clome closer to me. Please.
Why doesn't a single dog bark in the village?

I have fears lest someone come to pass here.
Night deepens over the castle.
Let this night be our own for once.

Let your arms be placed around my neck.
We are both young. O youth, be everlasting!

SEARED GRAPE LEAVES

Upon the dark sodden ground in the yard
The seared grape leaves fall
Silently, one by one.

Today as usual
I sweep them with a broom and weep.
When will this misery end?

Upon the dark sodden ground in the yard
The seared grape leaves fall
Silently, one by one.

Kim, Sang'yong (1902-1951)

Born in Yŏnchŏn, Kyŏnggi Province, Kim graduated from the English
Department of Rikkyo University in Japan. He taught at Ewha Women's Univer-
sity and at Yonsei University. He worked with *The Korea Times*, an English daily,
as an editorial writer. He began his literary career by publishing his poems in 1935
in *The Poetry Garden*. His works concern pastoral and nostalgic dreams of man.
His collected poems *Homesickness* came out in 1935.

I WOULD HAVE A WINDOW FACING SOUTH

I would have a window facing south
And patches of corn stretched in front.
I would hoe
And I weed with a spade.
I would stay here although
The cloud beckons me somewhere.
I would hear birds' melodies free.
You may come to my table.
When corn ripens enough.

Asked why I live here
I would just smile

THE HARBOR

Sorrow is eternal.
Waves dash against the sandbars.
Under the vast heaven
The lonely traveler is weary.

My eyes closed;
Memory looms near
Beyond the rim of sight.

I wonder if peace
Glows under the few lanterns there.

SNOWY MORNING

Snowy morning is
The holiest hour for prayer.

What beauty the ink black
Branches make on the impeccable
Hillside!

The pond breathes
Like a fresh-born babe.

Cockcrow far away,
How inviting the warmth
Of an eternal nest!

HOME THOUGHT

On a deserted mountain path,
pillowing on a stone,
I watch the sky

where clouds pass;
I long for my hometown
that does not exist.

Kim, Yŏngnang (1903-1950)

Born in Kangjin, South Chŏlla Province, Kim (his real name being Yunsik) studied English literature at Aoyama Academy in Japan. Along with Park Yong-ch'ŏl and Yi Ha-yun, Kim published his poems in *The Poetry Literature*. Kim seriously considered poetry as an art expressing the beauty of experience. He made a successful effort to polish the Korean language to serve his purpose. A stray bullet killed him during the Korean War. His work includes *Collected Poems of Kim Yŏngnang* (1935) and *Selected Poems of Kim Yŏngnang* (1949).

TILL PEONIES BLOOM

I will await my spring
till peonies bloom.
When the peonies drop their dead
I will lament over for their loss.

One day in May, a hot summer day
When all the peonies are gone,
petals stuck to the ground,
my vegetating desire crumbles to dust.

With my peonies gone my year ends.
And I must weep away the rest of the year.
I will await my spring, glorious yet sad,
till peonies bloom again.

AN ENDLESS RIVER

Somewhere in my mind
flows an endless river;
The waves silver and slippery
glide in the morning sun.
Somewhere in my heart,
in my eyes or in my veins
nestles my mind unseen.
Somewhere in my mind
Flows an endless river.

THE SUNSHINE WHISPERS TO THE STONE WALL

Like sunshine whispering to the stone wall,
like a brook grinning beneath the grass,
I wish to gaze on the sky all day long,
my heart glued to the sweet spring lane.

Like blushes on a bride's cheeks,
like gentle waves rippling a Muse's heart
I wish to gaze on the silken sky,
the softened emerald that sails by.

ANYONE WHO UNDERSTANDS ME

If anyone understands me,
Understands my heart as I do,
I will give him my secret treasures:
The dust that settles on my heart;
The tear-drops, tender and pure;
The dew-drops crystallized in the clear night.

How I long for him
Who will understand me as I do!
Could I see him far off in dreams?

Love may burn like
A perfumed jade in flames.
But my heart, dimmed and smudged,
Knows not what love is.

MAY

A path from the field ends in a flowering village.
A lane out of the village leads to the greening field.
Endless rows of crops wave in the wind;
The sunlight slants upon each row,
Barleys baring their shameless fat waists,
Their wings untried, the fledgling orioles
Chase each other for their mates.
The bright country lane dazzles the eyes.
O mountain peaks, preened and coquettish,
Where will you be for the night?

Park, Yongch'ŏl (1904-1938)

Born in Kwangju, South Chŏlla Province, Park studied German literature at Tokyo University of Foreign Studies. As a member of *The Overseas Literature* school, he stood for the purity and independence of arts against the politically oriented literature of the leftists. The pure lyric movement championed by him brought about a turning point in the history of modern Korean poetry. In 1930 Park initiated and financed *Poetry* and in 1931 *Literature Monthly* and again in 1933 *Literature*, all of which served the purpose of advocating and propagating his creed. *Complete Works of Park Yongch'ŏl* was published in 1939.

THE DEPARTING BOAT

I must go now
Lest my youth be wasted in sorrow.

I must go now.
Should I leave this peaceful harbor
with equanimity
Those peaks and valleys
familiar to my feet,
Those wrinkled faces dear to my heart
staying in my eyes misted with tears?

Those who leave shall miss
Those left behind.
A fugitive looking back on his home.

The wind blows the cloud adrift
as I turn around.
Is there a shore to greet my landing?

I must go now
Lest my youth be wasted in sorrow.
I must go.

YOUR SHADOW

The sands lie stretched
white for miles.

Behind the cloud
is hidden a song.

Your shadow wavers dimly
in the haze.

I waste away thin and pale
in your thoughts.

COLD FOREHEAD

While I sit alone in the vast darkness
with a light burning bright, how loneliness
strikes me, totally deprived!

What a comfort if a spring of wild flowers
should keep me company!

Myself totally deprived,
The snow silently falls in sheets;
My whole frame burns phosphorescent green.
What a joy if the crickets
should keep me company!

When my frame burns in phosphorescent flame
my forehead cold and cleared will sense
every nerve cell move.

What a pleasure if a wish-fulfilling star
should be lodged in my heart!

Yi, Yuksa (1904-1944)

Born in Andong, South Kyŏngsang Province, Yi (his real name being Hwal) studied sociology at Peking University. He died in a Peking prison as a political prisoner connected with the underground activity for Korean independence. His common subjects concern nature. His works as a whole reflect an aristocratic taste with a dash of modernistic technique. *Collected Poems of Yi Yuksa* was published posthumously in 1946.

TWILIGHT

The curtain lifted, I will
Welcome you into my closet.
How lonely as sea gulls
Human beings are!

Twilight, give me your sure hands.
I will kiss them
With my burning lips
Let me kiss all that comes to my arms.

The stars glittering in the December constellation,
The nuns secluded amid booming bell-sounds,
The countless convicts on cement floors,
What fear twitches their lonely hearts!

While you hold in your arms those caravans
That ride camelback across the Gobi desert,
Those Africans bolting arrows from their shady jungle;
Leave to my burning lips the remaining half the world.

Twilight, come again tomorrow
And I will lift my green curtain
To invite you into my room, cozy in May.
You may come again
When you find your desire cooled.

THE GRAPES

Come July in my home town
grapes ripen into fruitfulness.

The legend of the town
hangs in clusters on vines.
The dreamy sky far out
comes to sink in each grape.

When the sky-blue sea above
bares her breasts and a white sailboat comes
gracefully to the shore
the guest dear to my heart will arrive,
way-worn, in a blue robe.

If he comes to share these grapes
why should I mind wetting my hands?

Boy, go and bring on the table
a silver tray and a white napkin.

THE VERTEX

Lashed by the scourge of a harsh season
I was driven at last to the north,

Where the bored heaven succumbed to the height
And the black frost cut my flesh.

I do not know where to stretch my leg;
where to land a single step.

No choice but to close my eyes and muse:
The winter here is a steel rainbow.

WILDERNESS

In the beginning of time
when heaven was first made
hardly was there any cockcrow.

When all the mountain ranges
rolled seaward in love
they dared not leave this place defiled.

Through eons of time
the busy seasons blew and blasted
until a big river sprang into flowing.

Snow falling, a whiff of aroma floats
from plum blossoms somewhere around;
I sow the seeds of my humble song.

In eons of time hence
a superman will come on a prancing white horse.
Let him chant my song to echo in this wilderness.

FLOWERS

The sky reaches its limit in the east.
No drop of rain falls
And yet flowers blaze in flames.
What endless days I have dreamed of my life!

When the day dawns cold upon the tundra
Flower-buds stir in deep snow
For the days when the swallows will come in flocks:
The never-to-be-broken promise.

Amid whirling waves,
In a citadel aflame in the wind,
Dreamers, like so many enchanted butterflies,
I call you from this far-off place.

Kim, Kwangsŏp (1905-1977)

Born in Kyŏngsŏng, North Hamgyŏng Province, Kim majored in English at Waseda University, Japan. Affiliated with *The Overseas Literature* school, he began his literary career in the early 1930's by introducing Korea overseas literature in translation. He was also active in promoting theatrical arts in their infancy at the time. Like many of his contemporaries, he published his poems in *The Poetry Garden*. *Longing* (1938), his first book of poems, epitomizes the general mood of the age against the backdrop of agony. His work includes *Longing* (1938), *Heart* (1949), *The Sunflower* (1958), *The Pigeons at Songbukdong* (1969) and *Social Reaction* (1972).

THE DOVE IN SŎNGBUKDONG*

The city growing with a new lot number assigned
to the hilly area in Sŏngbukdong, the dove,
the original resident, has forfeited its abode.
Continually scared by the explosions from a quarry
its heart has been cracked in the end.
And yet it wings in a circle over the old habitat,
over the community against the blue morning sky
fresh as God's square
as if to bring blissful word to the people.
In the barren ravine in Sŏngbukdong
no patch of ground is left for it
on which to land and peck a grain or two.
And yet wherever it goes
it can hardly escape the explosions
blowing up rocks in the quarry
and it finally has taken refuge on a rooftop.
Whelmed by nostalgia at the sight of smoke
it wings back to the quarry assigned a lot number Hill 1
to dip its bill in the warmth of a rock
that's been split apart.

* Used to be a suburban area of Seoul.

Once it looked upon man as a saint.
Friendly to man it loved as he did;
like man it enjoyed freedom.
Once the symbol of love and peace,
it's forfeited its hill and man at the same time
and is left homeless incapable of evoking
the very idea of love and peace.

HEART

My heart is the calm waves,
Shaken easily in the breeze,
Shaded by a passing cloud.

Some people throw stones;
Others fish in it;
Still others sing.

When the shore gets deserted at night
The stars sail quietly on the waves;
The woods lull them
To sleep, silent.

I dream every night
For fear swans should come
To disturb the waves.

A SUMMER MORNING AFTER A SHOWER

The day after a shower
The clear sky sinks into the pond
To cast a summer morning

Where a gold fish
Scrawls his poem
On the deep blue sheet.

SOLITARY CELL No. 66

In the evening
Outside the dingy windowpanes
Crusted with hoary frost-work
Wind blows incessantly;
Magpies chatter.

The black screen is drawn
Across the sunless iron window to the north;
The shadow of a figure in scarlet
Stirs sadness in me
Under a lone lamp light.

Dampened by sighs,
The walls, chill and smudged,
May retreat any time tomorrow;
Cells in all make a row of graves.

Life breathes here.
Sympathy reciprocates.
When the wishful outlet opens a crack
The pearls lodged in the depth of the heart
Roll down to turn to tears.

Dark, day and night
In the iron window to the north;
Beyond the black screen
Wind blows incessantly.

PATHOS

The sea at night is endlessly dark,
A lamplight flickering in the dead center,

The waves break against the rocks under my feet.
Freedom echoes eternal sadness in this land.

The crying of gulls through the darkness far out
Laps on my ears and dies, tearing my heart's wound.

O bird of poetry, weeping in flight
Since you are fated to fly chartless in the dark,
Let the sorrow-chained poet go with you
To the sea of the night.

LONGING

All flowers of language
Turn to a mute orphan,
To a dream, to grief.

Something calls me.
I go adrift by the wind
In the starless night.

In the dark, oppressive
As in a nightmare,
One clear vision penetrates my whole being.

Yi, Hayun (1906-1974)

Born in Ichŏn, Kangwŏn Province, Yi studied English literature at Tokyo Politics-Economics University. An active member of *The Overseas Literature* school, Yi contributed toward introducing overseas literature mainly through translation into the Korean literary world. With Park Yongch'ŏl he co-edited *The Poetry Literature* in 1930 and *The Literary Monthly* in 1931. He taught at several universities including Seoul National University. His work includes *A Water Mill* (1939), *An Anthology of Modern Lyric Poems* (1939) and *Selection of French Poems* (1948) in translation.

DAISIES

I love daisies blowing in the fields.
Their lovely hue and scent I love.
I love them most because in solitude
They blow and fade in the fields.

I love poets of this country.
The poems they write I love because
They are true in hue and scent
Like lonely daisies blowing and fading
In the fields.

A WATER MILL

I drop my memory-petals one by one
Into the scoops of the turning wheel;
I see my memory burst into blossom
As each scoop empties itself.

While the wheel groans as it turns,
My heart caught in the days gone by
Fills with sighs and tears.

A grey-haired miller strains
His sight for something.
The mill thuds down upon the grain,
Water continually pouring down the wheel.

WATERS

Dead quiet while imprisoned in the pond
Waters chat along as they
Run across the shoals.

They hasten toward the ocean
Rinsing every pebble on the way
After sixty miles in the vales,
Ninety more miles across the fields,
They empty into the ocean in the end.

Imprisoned in the pond in the morning,
Half way across the shoals by day,
They steal at night into the ocean.

Silent and purring by day
They proceed mournfully all night through.

Shin, Sŏkchŏng (1907-1974)

Born of a family of literary tradition in Puan, North Cholla Province, a victim to the encroaching Japanese colonists, Shin moved to a remote village where he spent his boyhood. Though his family was physically impoverished, he was richly rewarded with the nature surrounding him—the picturesque scenery, a variety of wild flowers and rolling hills overlooking the sea dotted with islets. Engrossed in Buddhism, he was once torn between becoming a monk and otherwise. Deciding to be a farmer, he returned to his hometown to devote himself to writing. His first book of poems *The Candle Light* (1939) won him a special position as a pastoral poet. After the war he could no longer remain in the quiet of pastoral firmness. *The Glacier* shows him keeping in touch with everyday-world experience. His work includes *Candle Light* (1939), *The Sad Pastoral* (1947), *The Glacier* (1956), *Mountain's Overtures* (1967) and *Soughing in the Bamboo Grove* (1970).

IF YOU CALL

If you call
I will come to you
Like yellow gingko leaves
That drift in the autumn wind.

If you call
I will come to you
Like a new moon sinking quietly
On a night when mist settles over lake.

If you call
I will come to you
Like a stream that curves along
The sky-rim on warm spring days.

If you call
I will come to you
Like the early spring sun that seeps in the grass
When white herons chant in the azure sky.

IT IS NOT TIME YET TO LIGHT THE CANDLE

The slant rays of the setting sun feel sad;
Mother, it's not time yet to light the candle.
Aren't the little birds of my meditation
still flying in the blue savannah of sky?
When the sky grows apple-red
those little birds will return with dusk;
our little lambs on the slope lie down
on the old green couch to bask in the lingering sun.
At last evening fog settles on the serene lake.
But, Mother, it's not time yet to light the candle
for the old hill's meditative face hasn't faded yet;
one can hardly hear night's footfalls or its sable
skirt rustling against its own feet as it comes
out of the far-off forest.
The sound of waves lapping against the dyke dies away;
no wonder the crows visiting the country in late fall
have fled far away with the wind.
Now on your back the baby turns in his sleep
as if asking you to hum him to sleep again.
Mother, do not light the candle yet.
You will see a tiny star peeping out
in the sky beyond the timberline far out.

IN YOUR EYES

In your eyes
the fresh green of May
unlooses a sweet scent of white wild roses.

In your eyes
the twinkling stars
spin out their tales.

In your eyes
the sound of a bell rings in waves
from far away.

In your eyes
the warm hands wave promising
a reunion in far-off days.

In your eyes
joyful days are coming
when we can share our happy tales.

SAD DESIGN*

Heaven
and I
and green hills under heaven.
Nothing else.

No earth where a flower blooms.
No earth where a single bird comes to sing.
No earth on which a young deer rollicks around.

Night
and I
and millions of stars.
Nothing else.

Only the night drifts, jostled.
The darkness of night drifts and drifts.
What star in the night sky can soothe my mind?

* Written at the height of atrocities under Japanese colonial rule.

DO YOU KNOW OF THAT FAR-OFF LAND?

O Mother,
Do you know of that far-off land
Where young deer leap about,
White water fowls fly over the serene lake,
And red berries on wild briars blaze
A narrow path on the edge of an enormous forest?

O Mother,
Do you know of that far-off land
Where no one lives save the mournful sounds
Of the sea at a distance when
Dusk gathers in the wide cornfield,
And white lambs graze freely in the sun?
On our way back gentle down the slope
Remember we will drive the young flock homeward.

O Mother,
Do you know of that far-off land
Where the day gentle rain falls ceaselessly,
Pigeons fly far into the May sky,
You can hear calls of a pheasant.
Winter ravens soar over our heads
And yellow gingko leaves drift in mid-air.

Mother,
Won't we pick together those red apples
In that land when honey bees
Start to buzz in the sunny orchard?

Yu, Ch'ihwan (1908-1967)

Born in Ch'ungmu, South Kyŏngsang Province and educated at Yonsei University, Yu wandered in Manchuria during the war. After the liberation in 1945, he returned to his homeland and worked as a high school principal. Yu's work is tinged with metaphysical ponderings over life and nature. The incantatory tone of his language fascinates the sensitive ear. "The Flag" is one of the best remembered of his works. He was awarded the Korean Poets Prize (1946), the Seoul City Cultural Prize (1950) and the Free Literature Prize (1968). His work includes *Selected Poemsof Yu Ch'ihwan* (1939), *Collected Poems of Ch'ŏngma* (pen name) (1945), *Life Chapter* (1947), *A Blue Dragonfly's Diary* (1949), *With Infantry* (1953), *A Cock in Jerusalem* (1953) and *The Ninth Collected Poems* (1957).

WONDER IS WITH US

My boy is not back home till dark;
I walk out into the road to meet him.
A slice of moon slants
Dreamily at the road's edge.

Above my house lighted brightly under the elm
The Dipper shimmers like a mysterious sentinel.

Now we give in to illness
And then get pinched by poverty.
But we have harmony trickling into us
And the celestial host
Guard us every night;
The evanescence of our being
Is tied to the infinity of the universe.
My boy, come, we will go back home,
Hand in hand where the bright stars guide us.

HAPPINESS

Love to me is happier
Than to be loved.

Again today I write
At the post office window
That opens onto the emerald sky.

Through the street-facing door
People come, numberless, happy as they are,
To buy stamps or get telegram forms,
For a message, sad, glad, or kindhearted,
Bound for their homes or those they love.

Blown and driven in the wind
Of this care-thick world,
In the garden of dislocated humanity,
Our love, I pray, flowers into yearning.

Love to me is happier
Than to be loved.

Again today I cannot
Resist my urge to write.

O my love, I must bid you farewell.
Be it my last word of this world
Happy indeed I was
Because I loved.

ROCK

When I die, I shall be a rock.
Love and pity shall not touch,
not joy nor anger moves me.
Exposed to the slashings of weather
I will whip myself to withdraw inward
in eternal, impersonal silence
until life itself is lost to memory:
drifting clouds, distant thunder.
No song will I ever sing
even in dreams
nor will I weep in pain
though split in two.
I shall be a rock when I die.

THE TREE OF GOODNESS

By the roadside where I would roam stood an old pine
Spreading its dark limbs carelessly aloft into space.
Even when windless, the tree would sigh so sadly
I used to stop awhile beneath it, happy
To hitch my thoughts with the sound of the pine
To the edge of the distant sky.
One day I found the tree cut down mercilessly.

Although the realities of life tempt us to take
The wood for heat rather than the shade and the sound
I stand in its place holding my arms high up into the air;
But I know not how to make my palm make
The profound sound of the tree.
Notwithstanding the divine music that sounds
From the remote sphere above my head
I grieve over the loss of the good tree to prove it.

A KITE

A something that has come into being
Out of the swell of the sea,
A drop from the deep blue of the sky,
Little soul, how pure you are,
Soaring in the bright sky of July.

Too proud for the animal-obsessed earth,
Far from the worldly ties of love and relation,
Beyond the realm of man,
It sails in the immensity of heaven.

With its soul, bold yet cautious,
Quietly casting the anchor of meditation,
How it spreads its brilliant dreams aloft
Over the bright daylight world, O Kite.

FLAG

A voiceless shouting.
A handkerchief of eternal nostalgic drive
Waving into the distant blue of ocean.

Lofty ideal flutters, wave-like, in the wind.
Sorrow spreads its wings like a heron
On the staff of thought, pure and upright.

I wonder who first hoisted this aching heart
Of ours into the air.

IT WILL BE KNOWN IN THE END

It will be known in the end
To be a vast emptiness.
My life, like a wild flower,
Blooms and wilts unknown.
Groaning under the heaviness of grief
My life seems a mere gust of wind.
It is a patch of cloud
That floats briefly and vanishes.
We are not born twice into the world.
The night my life comes
To the end of its journey
O Sun and Moon, rise,
But disturb me not after death.
Let the bowls of billions of stars
Be the canopy of my tomb;
Insects in permanent secret,
Let your weeping be the everlasting
Lament for my death.
It will be known in the end
That we are a vast emptiness.

Shin, Sŏkch'o (1909-1976)

Born in Hansan, South Ch'ungchŏng Province, Shin studied philosophy at Hosei
University, Japan. His early poems show Valerian influence. Later he turned to
Taoist thought in search of classical form and poetics. Still later he absorbed
Buddhist thought into his work. His books of poems include *Collected Poems*
(1946), *The Gong Dance* (1959) and *The Song of Storm* (1970). He worked for a
daily newspaper as an editorial writer until his death in 1976.

FLUTE

How sad, cold moon!
Do you set to no purpose
Your remote dreams adrift
Onto the hazy ancient sky
Over the capital?

Though days and months have rolled
In and out since antiquity,
O moon, can't you end
The whirligig of life storms?

I wonder if a master musician
Could play on you, O flute,
To sweep away with your cosmic music
The clouds lowering over the blue ocean.

Over the ruins of decayed royalty
Reign the cold moon and haze.
O heart-breaking flute of silence!

CATAPULTING A STONE

Onto the ocean
Onto the infinite waves
I catapult a stone
As if to shoot an arrow into a void.

The stone flashes golden
As it raises a brief water spray
And disappears,
Traceless.

O ocean,
Where did you hide my arrow?

In the ocean
The infinite waves alone
Roll for endless miles.

THE GONG DANCE*

"Pleasure vanishes like morning dew"—*Siddharta*

Against my life-long wish to live
like an immaculate petal ·
what shall I do
with the doleful spring
that gushes out
from the deep woods of my heart?

Perhaps, it's like the sound of a bell
ringing from a remote temple in the green hill.
The bright moon is beaming in vain
on the empty temple;
a sleepless philomel weeps so sadly,
on a spray in the back yard.
Woe is me. What shall I do?
How I've been dreaming
of the Nirvana
of matchless joy
that I can keep to myself!
Nevertheless,
dizzying dust has gathered unawares
on the clean mirror of my mind.

Flesh is sad
A fault-ridden body of this temporal world.
The madding passion of this world
grips my body like a beast.

---

* A Buddhist ritual dance performed by a monk or nun while striking a brass gong
set up on the floor.
Note: The poem has more than one version. This translation is based on the one
included in *An Anthology of Buddhist Poems* (1973).

O this form, in such beauty.
In my treasure woods there's a path
running forever split between mind
and its enthralling body
where a hidden serpent wriggles.

Like a drifting cloud
quietly flows a stream
on which ripple down fallen petals.
How the rolling waters break into jewels!
What can ever stay the mighty flowing
before the stream empties into the blue sea?
How I envy that stream which flows freely at will!
Plum-blossoms blossoming white
under the moon,
I lie down alone
in nun's quarters
but I can hardly get to sleep
as if laden with cares.

O dizzying concerns of this world.
What resignation for show!
Are the eight commandments and hymns for nothing?
O fruits of illusion born of human fate!
In the white jade skin hidden from sight,
lies the sad abyss of soul
I dream of.
O honeyed dew on the petals.
O heart-rending rapids
that rush down out of control.
O spring of my heart
that runs forever undrained.

So fleeting are the cataracts of flowers.
There's a sobbing in my beautiful ravine;
on the quiet flow of my frame,
on the dashing currents of change
I shall end in drifting
idly like fallen petals.

Is it this very suffering flesh
that is only real?
This very self that exists for a brief period,
this frame that flows flooded with use of life,
a mere flower-bud that burns with pure desire,
an illusory butterfly worn with cares.

Far from the dust of this wide world
I have my eyebrows slightly arched
under my hood, tilted low.

This green shaded robe is kept spotless
free from a patch of shame.
The empty hill lies dotted with lilies
that ail in secret;
arrow-roots running wild,
the moon shines brightly.
In the dead of the night
in the quiet of my upper room
I hear nothing but the dinning sound of water.
No other soul in sight but a lone candle-light
by which my neck band and my long-sleeved robe
are shed to ripple into a long-drawn sigh.
Like a dancing moth drawn to a flame
I chase a dream, sweet and endless.

Alas! Does solitude sire
a sinful serpent of thought?
O Maya that rises in quietness from the deep of my mind.
O dreaming Maya that rises inwardly.

On the myriad-folded ranges of mountains
arrow-roots, twined and tangled,
run wild and free to wrap tightly
around an alder, slim and straight.
Are men also born to live tangled
and free like that?
For me
I have no wish or attachment left in me

For I am a mere flower that blooms by nature.
This frame of mine that has grown big
charmed by the full-blown blossoms,
a sheer mass of roses.
Behold the hill where peach and plum blossoms
swirl in midair.

O seeds of evil chained to the eight phases of being.
How hard to cut off stubborn affinity
clinging to the three worlds!*
I wish to wander madly in the dream woods
assigned to me for a living
but I do not know whither to go
like a sailor beaten unconscious by the storm.

O my Bodhisattva,
Bodhisattva!
Save us, gracious Bodhisattva!
Save us, merciful Bodhisattva!
Save us, compassionate Bodhisattva!

Under the dome of boundless cosmos,
under the dome of boundless cosmos
My body is but a flower that blows and blasts,
I wish to live sheltered in the cloud-capped mountains,
sheltered in the cloud-capped mountains.
And yet, and yet,
I still dream of the temporal world,
fascinated by the demon.

O demon, demon,
wild beast of worldly passions.
Caged in a tile-roofed dungeon,
face to face with a cold gilt image
I writhe prostrate on the floor,
captive to the anguish of this world;

*The world of desire-driven beings, the world of beings with form, and the world
of being without form.

the fire flaring up under my sable robe
is like incense that curls up
from a flowery fumigator.

In the small hours of the night when wind-bells
tinkle faintly in the wayward wind,
flowering sprays sway in a dance
against the casement of the abbot's quarter;
night seems wearing further on;
the very cranes doze in the cloud yard.
Left alone to myself in the cold of a cell
I quietly shed my long-sleeved robe;
rumpled in folds on the floor
it resembles a lotus-bloom
that floats on the blue water in a pond.

Can I get to sleep if I lie down
or dispel sadness if I sit to rest?
I stay up all night couching in the woods
of withering worries.
The road to the West chills me even in dreams;
mist darkens the vale coated with eons of time.
Where is the paradise?
I do not so much as know whither I am going.

O Enlightened One, born of exalted Brahman,
How your mind illumines like gold!
The ocean-wide mercy of yours.
The lily-tender touch of yours.
Oh, the desire of flesh sucked into the region
of honeyed oblivion.
Look how the cataract tumbles a thousand feet
down to the cloud-thick pond.

Let me go along,
all the miseries of this world
loaded on the back of my soul.

Shall I throw a surplice around my shoulders,
around my shoulders to dance
while I strike the gong?
Shall I throw a surplice around my shoulders,
around my shoulders to and lie down
and hold the wanton moon that's slipped out of clouds
in the folds of my robe that drapes loose my empty heart?
I only wish to go in peace through this painful night,
through this painful night.

Alas, am I mad?
or have I become a beast?
A beast of the demon?
Or a lustful doe descended to this world?
Woe is me. I must be mad.
Let me shake off temptation.
Pleasure vanishes like morning dew.
O dizzying thoughts!
False senses!
Open sandy fields
rolled in and out by the waves!
The wind of regret blowing,
my heart goes hollow like a cave.
On the hillslope where flowers wilt
weeps a philomel
whose songs alone
mingle mournfully in the sound of flowing waters
rending the heart of a sleepless soul.

I push the window open to the moon,
its halo rimming hazily around the tinted clouds.
The moon is moored low
over the roof-edge that tilts heavenward;
vedant hills high and low enwrap me.

And all around is nil in dead quiet.
O Nightingale, you weeping philomel,
In what part of the clouds are you crying
throughout the night?

The sound of rushing waters seems
choked with sorrow, muffled by your cry.

Way off in the bushes by the brook
I undress myself and lave my fair body.
The empty hill and the moon shattered in the water
sail afloat down the gilt surface of the water,
Fair is its image dunked in the shallows;
a string of creamy jewels scattered on the water-glass
only to gather into shape.
Unable to flow like water
it has to stay inside the cloud-rim
like the moon sunk into the water.

Bubble-like mountains locked in form!
I have come this far
to wash myself clean of the dust of sin.
Silence settles like a green veil;
in the specular beauty of the glittering image
the latent force of illusion comes to surface.
Alas!
Are mind and body at war everlastingly?
How the form of concept remains for ever undefined!

O water! O flowing water! O overflowing water!
What a bliss that your body is broken loose!
Never to be hardened into form, your body is free
from worldly desires and sorrow.
Down the jewel vale that spokes in myriad directions
you flow freely out of the deep mountains
as the prime cause of lasting freshness,
as the pure fount that goes forever unpolluted.

Gong,
goes the bell at dawn;
night is about to end.
Gong, gong, goes the bell.
The peal of the bell rolls in waves
to echo the flowing water.

Look. I stand upright in the clean wash of glass.
What a lonely being I am!

Dawn brings all into their distinct form,
taking substance apart from image.
The moon casts a dim shadow
on the purpling woods.
The blue heaven lightening,
green peaks come near like a tower.
The rocks shooting up through the clouds
and ever-vegetating trees all
come to life from the darkness,
giving off immortal light.
May you stay with me forever.
From the blue peaks up in the distance
Comes in a surge an ocean of bright woods,
the thick forest flapping its gilded wings.
The morning sun spreads like roses about to open
and the birds asleep on the twigs
wake up to warble in joyous notes.

Ding, ding, beats the drum.
Ding, ding, dong, beats the drum for the morning rite.
"Merciful Buddha" intones the prayer.
In robe and prayer beads strung around my neck
I perform rites for the morning.
O horde that bows to an idol!
O sad hypocrites!
O false female believers!

Sound of drum   sound of prayer
sound of prayer   sound of water
sound of water   sound of gong
sound of gong   sound of water
The sound of water flows
to ring the bell in waves.

In the countless columns of cloud
echoes the sound of the mountains.

The gentle wind that unlocks my heart
now passes through the rose bush
that carpets the slopes of remote mountains.
Letting my sleeves flow loose
I come down from the quiet of the temple;
I come down from the worthless vale of sorrow.

Yi, Sang (1910-1938)

Born in Seoul, Yi (his real name being Kim, Haegyŏng) studied architecture in high school. Because of t.b., he quit his position as architect and launched into a disorderly life; the so-called *fin-de-siecle* malady struck him. His behavior as well as his writing against convention came as a shock to his contemporaries. He was the first to employ the surrealistic technique rooted in psychological realism. He wrote *A Crow's-eye-view* (1934) and *The Complete Works of Yi Sang*.

MIRROR

No sound in the mirror.
No world is that quiet.
I have ears in the mirror too,
two pitiful ears
that cannot hear my own voice.
I am left-handed in the mirror,
left-hander unable to shake hands.
I cannot touch myself in the mirror
because of the mirror,
but how could I ever meet myself
in the mirror
but for the mirror?
Though I have no mirror in me
there is always *I* in the mirror.
I do not know for sure but the mirror *I*
is engaged in his one-sided struggle.
The mirror *I* is my reversal.
The resemblance of the two is remarkable.
I feel extremely sorry that I cannot worry about
or examine myself in the mirror.

THE MORNING

The dark air does harm to the lungs.
Soot deposits on the surface of the lungs.
I suffer from a fever all night long.
What countless nights I have had!
I drag them in and out forgetting daybreak.
Morning lights the lungs, too.
I look around to see if anything is missing
From the night.
I find the habit back again.
Quite a few pages have been torn
From my luxurious volume.
The morning sunbeams write in so many words
To conclude the worn-out pages
As if the noiseless night world would not come any longer.

POEM No. 12

Dirty linen pieces in a bundle fly into the air and drop to the
ground, a flock of white pigeons. The
leaflet the size of a hand says war is over
the other side of the sky and peace has come.
The flock of pigeons was the clean linen. This
side of the sky the size of a hand dirty war is
started to club the white pigeons to death. When the
air is tainted with soot the flock of pigeons flies
into the other side of the sky the size of a hand.

THE CLIFF

No flower is in sight. It is fragrant.
The fragrance bursts open. I dig a grave there.
The grave is not in sight, either. I sit down
in the invisible grave. I lie down. Again
the flower is fragrant. The flower is not in
sight. The fragrance bursts open. Forgetful, again
I dig a grave there. The grave is not in sight.
I enter the invisible grave forgetful of the
flower. True, I lie down. Ah, ah. Fragrance is
the flower—the flower, invisible, unseen.

A FLOWER-TREE

In the midst of wilderness stands a flower tree,
no other tree near it. It blossoms in passion as
much as it yearns for its companion somewhere.
Yet it cannot near its fellow tree it is so much
in love with. I run away toward another tree
as if I were the very flower tree.

Mo, Yunsuk (1910-1990)

Born in Wŏnsan, South Hamgyŏng Province, Mo went to Ehwa Women's University where she studied English. Along with No, Ch'onmyŏng, Miss Mo distinguished herself as a major woman poet. While No's concerns are grief and bitterness and thwarted hope in life, Mo's poems project a bright outlook on life. Her passion for her homeland is legendary. Her work includes *The Bright Zone* (1933), *Wren's Elegy* (1938), *A Jade Hairpin* (1947), *The Waves* (1951), *Collected Poems* (1974) and *Collected Poems* (1979). *Wren's Elegy* and *The Pagoda*, an epic poem and sixty poems were published in 1980 in New York (in English translation).

WHAT A FALLEN SOLDIER SAYS*

I chanced on a fallen soldier while wandering the hills and valleys
in a suburb south of Seoul.—

In a solitary mountain valley
I see a lone soldier lying,
wordless, motionless,
his eyes closed skyward.

In khaki uniform, badges sunlit on the shoulders,
he is the pride of the Republic, a second lieutenant.
Blood is still gushing out of his heart;
it smells more pungent than roses.
I lean over him to lament his youthful death
and listen to what he has last to say:

I have died young at five and twenty,
gone as a son of the Republic.
Fallen in a brave fight to defend my country
against the enemy invading like stormy clouds.

With my rifle, firm in hand,
shrapnel-proof helmet shielding my head,
I have never been a coward before the enemy,
Oh, no.

* Based on the poet's experience during the Korean War.

At the call of a greater inner voice in me
I dashed over the hills, vales, thorny bushes
and mounds of the dead.
Like Admiral Yi Sunsin, like Napoleon, like Caesar

I advanced day and night to save the nation
from disaster.
I fought to put the enemy to rout.
I wanted to march farther than the sky-limit.
I wanted to sweep them off as if in a storm.

Mother and father I have, and dear brothers, too.
And a sweet girl I love.
A budding youth of this land,
I wished to share my flowering life with those I love.
I wished to grow singing with those birds on the wing.
And I fought bravely and died.
No one knows of my death.
O my country, my love!
How the gentle wind caresses me to dry
the sweat on my brow, on my lifeless brow!
How those stars comfort my soul at night!

Dressed in the uniform of the fatherland,
I shall lie down on the grass of this vale,
setting my tired body in peace.
I shall breathe the air that fills the sky.
I fought with pride for the country dear as my mother
and died an honorable death for the nation.
Fallen dead in this obscure valley,
I shall keep eternal company with those nightingales
that weep in the dew-laden grass at night.

O wind! You nameless birds!
When you meet my poor countrymen,
give this word of mine that I ask them
to weep not for me but for the fatherland.
Birds winging freely from the spring land,

when you meet my beloved girl by any chance
at a windowside while you fly,
go and tell her to weep not over my death
but for the glory of the Republic.
O my country, my countrymen, my sweet girl.

I go now for your happiness, leaving you
with my wish unfulfilled.
Defeat the enemy once and for all
and comfort my spirit and make up for my lost youth.
Turning back is shame worse than surrender or slavery.
Let others step out if they will.

But our Republican army,
you must fight it out till victory is won
and die in glory for this nation to prosper.
Once lost, the fatherland shall not be regained.
Look, O my country, how the storm arises!

Packs of wolves and lions charge down the hills and vales.
Will you dismiss this sorrow as mere sting of destiny?
No. It cannot be our destiny. Or let it be so,
for we are mightier than destiny. We really are.
Friends, destroy it, another enemy, with your brawny arms
with blood and soul handed down to us by our ancestors.

Fight when you must;
die when you must
to save the nation on the brink of perdition.
And let my wishes be known: Be it for the good
of the nation,
I'd gladly refuse to be put into the simplest coffin,
to lie buried in the grave.
Let the wild wind flail my frame;
let maggots feast on my flesh.
I shall be a handful of dust in the vale of my country.

In a solitary mountain valley
I see a lone soldier lying,

wordless, motionless,
his eyes closed skyward.

In khaki uniform, badges sunlit on the shoulders,
he is the pride of the Republic, a second lieutenant.

Blood is still gushing out of his heart;
it smells more pungent than roses,
I lean over him to lament his youthful death
and listen to what he has last to say.

THIS LIFE

If you call, I will come running.
Though I have no gold sash to adorn my skirt,
Though I have no pearls to inlay my shawl,
I will come, if you call.

I will live, if you want me to.
Though food runs short in the store-house
Or heavy debts throw me out of wits,
I will live, if you want me to.

I will die, if my death pays.
I will pass you by empty-handed.
If you want it, I will not spare my life.
I will drain my whole blood for you
What would I not give if only it could
Strengthen your frail limbs?
How can I go with your hands going pale?
How can I go with your knees going weak?

THE BRIGHT ZONE

Like ten thousand arrows shot into the air
The distant days ahead dance in our heart.
In this blessed zone where silver breeze ripples
Our life shall last forever.

You and I are of one ancestor of the same blood,
scions of the land of morning calm.
We march along the bank of the clean stream
That shines in the morning sun.

The melody of paradise mellows in the vineyard.
The stars rising at twilight these four thousand years
Alight on the graves from their infinite habitat.
Cows and horses idly follow the cowherd.

The mountain peaks and quiet streams fascinate
Travelers to stop on their way.
My country restful as a fairy land,
You are the breast of my eternal woman.

The fair climate above gives us a shelter in the land
Wide and fertile earth under is our glory.
O how shines the land; be peace with thee.
Be our lives true and everlasting also.

Like ten thousand arrows shot into the air
Distant days ahead dance in our heart.
In this blessed zone where silver breeze ripples
Be the life of twenty million souls everlasting.

Kim, Kirim (1909-19 ??)

Born in Sŏngjin, North Hamgyong Province, North Korea, Kim studied English
literature at Tokyo University, Japan. As the first champion of the modernist po-
etry movement in Korea, Kim was reported missing during the Korean War, pos-
sibly forced into North Korea. He taught at colleges before the war. His books are
The Sun's Custom (1936), *The Weather Chart* (1939) and *The Sea and the Butterfly*
(1949).

THE WORLD IN THE MORNING*

* the first of the 7-part Weather Chart poem

The channel
is alive as sleek
as the snakeback
covered in
bristling scales.
Young mountain ranges are draped in colorful Arabian costumes.

The wind spreads smoothly over the shore like Saracen silk.
The haughty landscape lies stretched on the height of 7 a.m.

On the hills gasping for breath
the rusty bell-toll from a church
starts spraying ancient perfume.
Calves must be taking to the fields.
The girl today as usual sends off a sea-addicted steamship.

A railway station near the border.
An international train stamps its feet
impatient for the conductor's signal.
Each window
swallows up "good-byes" with women's drawn faces
framed in sobbing tears.
Airliners disperse like dust into the Continental air.

A gentleman's family go on a journey to Geneva
to test the effect of radio transmission from home.
Champagne. The deck. "Bon voyage." "I won't be gone for long."
The crew return to their positions
leaving their sighs to the steam whistles.

Multi-colored tapes flutter caught on the pierside
A colorful ribbon on a woman's hair.

Carrier pigeon
from the cabin-roof
have flown homeward to the capital city.

. . . 5 km on the sea . . . east of Sumatra . . . the party free from
colds . . . approaching the equator . . . 10 a.m. on the 20th

THE SEA AND THE BUTTERFLY

Since no one has ever told her
how deep the sea is
the white butterfly has
no fear of the sea.

She lands on the sea taking it
for a patch of blue radish;
she comes home like a princess,
her wings wet in the salt waves.

In the month of March the sea doesn't bloom
and the pale moon chills the thin waist
of the sad butterfly.

HOMESICKNESS

Way beyond the mountains and clouds
nestles my home village where there's
often a rumor about what's going on
in Russia across the border.

Suddenly, I stop short to hear
in the evening wind that rustles
in the roadside trees
someone calling a calf home.

SPRING

April at last wakes up
like a lazy leopard,
glittering,
itching for motion,
blood-curdling,
and arching its back
before it strives over the winter.

Kim, Kwanggyun (1912-)

Born in Kaesŏng, Hwanghae Province, Kim was one of the faithful adherents of
Kim, Kirim in championing the modernist movement in poetry. Affiliated with
Siin-burak (Poet's Village) he was more successful with his word-painting than
his predecessor. His work includes *Gaslight* (1939), *The Port of Call* (1947) and *A
Twilight Song* (1960).

SKETCH OF AN AUTUMN DAY

Fallen leaves are the bank-notes of the Polish
    government in exile.
They remind me of an autumn sky spread over the bombed-
    out city of Turon.
The road like a rumpled necktie fades
    into the cataracts of sunlight.
The 2 p.m. express races across the plains
    puffing up cigarette smoke into the air.
The factory roofs flash their teeth
    between the ribs of poplar trees.
Beneath a cellophane cloud sways in the wind
    a crooked wire fence.
Kicking through the grass alive with
    chirping insects
I catapult a stone into the air as if to shake
    the gloom of thought off my chest;
It sinks, drawing a parabola,
    beyond the screen of a slanting landscape.

LAMP

An insect cries
Silver-plating the moonlight in tender grief,
Its lean limbs waving.
I enter the room
And blow out the light.
A steam whistle, husky,
Cuts through the invading
Darkness in the distance.
My heart, battered and empty;
My pillow soaked,
The insects pour its scream all night
Onto the darkening ceiling,
Onto grey slide doors
And into my dismal dreams.

GASLIGHT

The pale gaslight hangs against the empty sky.
Where does its sad signal beckon me to go?
The long summer day hastens to fold its feathers.
Rows of towering buildings dip in the twilight
like so many bleached gravestones.
The glaring nightscape falls in a tumble
like weeds going wild and thoughts
have lost their utterance, dumb.
The darkness seeps in my skin.
A shouting in a strange street
brings foolish tears to my eyes.

Driven in the stream of hollow crowds
I do not know why the lengthening shadow
darkens as in hell
as if I caused this weight of grief.
Where does this sad signal beckon me to go?
The pale gaslight hangs against the empty sky.

THE SEA BREEZE

Wearing a mist-limp hat
I sadly watch the antique season.
A lone whistle sound is tossed behind.
Dark threads of rain sprinkle
On the fallen leaves on the pavement.
The hollow shadow of business quarters
Rims the old street battered like a steam boat.

Boat passing on the seas
Puffs out a white homing instinct.
The gulls waving handkerchiefs far away
Dot glittering flower-patterns
In the glow of twilight.

I sit on the shore of a nondescript port
My wooden shoes dipping in the surf
And send afloat the autumn of my crumbled youth
On the wing of the scudding salt wind.

FOREIGNERS' VILLAGE

In a paling glow of sunset
A carriage, a green lantern hanging in front,
Dwindles into a picturesque hamlet
Nestled lonely in the lap of a hill.

Over the top of a telegraph pole
Erected on the ridge overlooking the sea
A thin tissue of cloud passes,
Tinted in the crimson evening glow.
Weatherbeaten, each house
Has its windows shuttered.
Under a bridge overgrown with sedges
A little stream tinkles.

On the bench in a misty flower-garden
Is scattered a bunch of mirthful laughter
With wilted flowers left by little girls
In the daytime.

AT THE NOKDONG GRAVEYARD

Has he come this far only to be buried in the red clay?
Here lie rows and rows of desolate mounds of the dead.
Sprawling, turfless, flowerless; without a single
Tree or a hillock for a shade.
The rain-soaked awning sobs in the wind.
And the bell tolls in waves in the empty wilderness.
Clutching at his thirty-eight years of sorrow
Have his shoulders been freed at last from their perennial
burden?
Alas!
Shall we part here, and is that all?
The sound of the hammer nailing the thick board
And the coffin lowering by the rope
Pierce through my temples.
Upon the small gravestone,
Upon my tightened lips,
The chill rain drips incessantly.

THE SILVER SPOON

The hill merges with darkness.
The evening glow fades.
My child is not at table for supper.
A silver spoon lies on his soft seat.
Tears well up at the spoon.

Wind rises in the deep night.
I hear my child laugh in the wind.
He looks into the room.
He opens the window and closes it.
I see him walk on a lane
Into the far-off field.

He steps slowly, crying, barefooted.
I call him but no response.
I see his shadow flicker.

No, Ch'ŏnmyŏng (1913-1957)

Born in Chang'yŏn, Hwanghae Province, No began writing while she was at
Ehwa Women's University. Affiliated with *The Poetry Garden*, No distinguished
herself as a rare talent and a great woman poet. Single all her life through, No
made her solitude and self-torture her weapon against the hostile universe. In *The
Song of Deer* she outgrows the nettling solitude and introspection and enters the
world of love and repentance. Her work includes *The Coral Reefs* (1938), *The
Window Side* (1945), *Looking at the Stars* (1953), *The Song of Deer* (1959) and
Complete Works by No Ch'ŏn-myŏng (1960).

WATCHING THE STARS

As a tree tilts heavenward
So we must go watching the stars overhead,
Though our feet kick dust on the ground.
What if you should be placed
Higher than the next fellow?
What if your name should be made
Greater than those of others?
What if you should take revenge on your enemy?
All end in trifles
Not worth a penny for a drink.
We must go ahead watching the stars overhead
Though our feet kick dust on the ground.

LONGING

My heart is on fire,
burning ceaselessly for something.

I reach out my hand, waving far into the distance.
Forgetting that my hands and feet are in chains,
I gasp in a desperate self-struggle.

Who was it that played flute once?
I do not know where its notes still
linger, here or there.

There must be some place that calls me;
Somewhere in the far distance
something seems to beckon.

My heart is burning, burning ceaselessly.

DEER

That long neck of yours
makes you a sad creature.

Always quiet and gentle
with the fragrant crown
You must come of a noble tribe.

Watching your own image
mirrored in the stream
you like to reminisce about the lost legend.
Lost in irresistible nostalgia
you crane your sad neck
to gaze at the faraway hills.

WILD CHRYSANTHEMUMS

How lonesome autumn would look
Without thee on the sloping hill in the fields!

Though no one would call thee a queen,
Thou hast refused the glory of spring garden.
Damsel of the deserted fields, thou alone,
Mixed in nameless weeds, keepst watch
Over the lonesome season.

Charmed by thine heart softer than reed-plumes,
I have brought thee home an armful with care and
Put in a vase with a prayer that thou grow there full and free.
But the freshness of the field was leaving thee day after day;
Smileless, thy face began to droop;
Thy splendor hast faded, in petal after petal.
Isn't vaseful of fresh water poured every
Morning worth a singledew-drop in the wilderness?
O I should have left thee there to grow and blow
Free in thy familiar soil.

Full of remorse
I take thee out in my trembling arms to bury
Thee under the blue sky in a cool corner of a hill-slope.
Wild chrysanthemum,
Thou hast there thy blue heaven;
Here is for thee the soft cushion, reed-plumes.

BEHIND BARS

I hear a dog's barking.
It cheers me up like a familiar voice.
Perhaps someone lives near.

I hear a dog's barking,
A sign of a happy family,
Shoes arranged neatly in the doorway.

In the early morning
Kitchen steams warm with cooking.
Soup sizzles over the brazier,
Who cares if grandmother complains?
The barking at dawn
Transmits a breath of family life.
The world outside is pure happiness
To those dumped behind bars.

THE GRAVEYARD

Leaves were about to turn red
When one early morning I visited
The graveyard with an armful
Of golden chrysanthemums.

You have gone this way
Never to return.

More than sad, my heart aches;
Wooden grave signs are scattered
Like mornful notes.

Kim, Hyŏnsŭng (1913-1976)

Born in Pyŏng'yang, North Korea and brought up in Kwangju, South Chŏlla Province, Kim studied at Sungsil College. His literary career started in 1934 when he was a student at collge. His life is divided into three periods: the first one was concerned with the physical world, morning, dawn, trees, and the like; the second, with a search for the inner world; the third, with the theme of loneliness as an essential part of human existence. Kim taught at Sungjŏn University. His work includes *Selected Poems of Kim Hyŏnsŭng* (1957), *A Defender's Song* (1963), *The Solid Solitude* (1968), *The Absolute Solitude* (1970) and *The Complete Works of Kim Hyŏnsŭng* (1974).

A HYMN TO LIFE

What of a life of struggle?
Could we after death bring the lovely
Evenings any earlier on the earth?

When our names are listed
In a widow's memorandum
And a bunch of unknown poets recite
Their pieces in our memory
In the hall the day after Friday . . .

What of a life of uncertainty?
How beauteously after death the wild flowers
Will flare up, dream-like, where we used to walk!
The birds of passage may come in season
To alight on our graves.

All that we treasure in a lifetime
Is like clouds in the sky.
Drifted away, heirless—the sigh, the despair,
The hunger, the laugh and even our love.

Beyond the attachments and pretensions
Of this world, the path open to us
To eternity is a prayer that our life
Be enduring, joyful and sad
After we are dead.

THE WINDOW

To say we love the window
Dazzles us less than to say
We love the sun.

If the window is lost
The channel to the sky is lost.

Brightness of spirit,
The foremost news for today.

The time we brighten the window
Is the time we can hum a song—
stars dwell in the far-off country
of December.

By keeping the window brightened
We can admit brightness into our eyes;
Let our bright eyes
Brighten our mind
For the days to come.

PRAYER IN AUTUMN

Let me pray alone in autumn.
Make me rich with your gift,
The humble mother tongue,
When leaves start to fall.

Let me love alone in autumn;
Choose but one single soul.
Let me fertilize this hour
To bear the choice fruit.

Let me alone
So that my soul may have peace
Like a bird that rests on a dry twig
After crossing the swelling ocean
And the valleys of lilies.

A SYCAMORE

Have you a dream?
I ask you, sycamore.
O I see your head already wet in the blue.

A world apart from yearning,
You seem to possess something
With which to spread your shade.

When I am alone and lonely
On a long weary way
You keep me company all through.

I wish I could blow my own soul
Into yours; we are no God, though.

The day we part company
At the end of our weary journey
I fear if there is a rich soil somewhere
That greets you.

I wish only to be your dutiful guardian
To keep you sheltered in a place
Into which I can open my window
And see the shining stars.

THE HORIZON

Where my vision ends
Its nucleus turns to cloud

Where my speech ends
its meaning rings, amplified

Life-long sorrow and pains
condense into a longing;
The loudest whistling on earth becomes
a mere scream of a winging wild duck

Every fragment of time past,
every slice of memory,
I will put up on the distant horizon,
watching them tinted in the setting sun

THE ABSOLUTE SOLITUDE

Now at last I've come to touch
the remote edge of eternity

On that edge I rub my eyes
to awake from my long sleep

From my fingertips
the everlasting stars scatter, their light
gone from my fingertips;
I feel anew the body heat
that comes closer to me

Through this heat
I alone embrace my eternity
that ends in me

And from my fingertips
I set adrift like so much dust
the wings of my words lined with soft dreams

I stroke again and again
with my wrinkled hands
the beautiful eternity that ends in me

And at my fingertips that can reach no farther
I keep silent in the end—with my own poems.

Chang, Manyŏng (1914-1976)

Born in Yon'baek, Hwanghae Province, Chang went to an English language school in Japan. Instead of attending classes, however, he used to stray into the library or into second-hand bookstores. Unlike many of his contemporaries, he turns to the natural world for his material. Chang sings the unstained beauty of nature and purity of childhood dreams. "Homesick," "Lamb," "The Child" were well accepted by critics. His work includes *Lamb* (1937), *Festival* (1939), *A Song for Childhood* (1948), *Night's Romance* (1956), *The Evening Bell-sound* (1957), *The Milestone* (1958) and *Collected Poems of Chang Manyong* (1964).

THE PROSTITUTE

Because she was unaware
That the t.b. bacteria were mercilessly
Motheating into her peach chest,
She did not lament over her body
Going ice-cold.

An old story.
She had lost her garment of chastity,
Her flesh smeared with scribbling
By so many males savage as cannibals.

No remorse. No sadness, either.
Now age, a crumpled map,
Hangs on her face like a chronology.
Once she thought of gardening
In the countryside. Her dream.
Once she waited for a princely gentleman
To enter the ruined fortress of her flesh.
Her last happiness.

One winter day, cold as realities of life,
The prostitute died old
In the servant quarters in a back alley of Seoul.
Her neighbors sent her a chill sneer
For her funeral. Not a single candle.

RAIN

Listen, Sunhee.
Come April when nightingales sing in the backwoods
Rain comes stepping gently on the green grass.

Rain shines her eyes like crystal
And sports her pearl necklace.

Rain weaves her silver lace all day long
In the shade of a weeping-willow.

Rain braves kissing me in daylight,
Her lips stained red with strawberries.

Gently humming rain brings home
The cherry-sweet twilight.
Rain tells not where to rest for the night.

Listen, Sunhee.
When we burn a candle, sitting together
Face to face,
We will hear rain chatting outdoors far into night
Until morning finds her gone out of sight.

HOMESICK

I walk seaward.
Evening glow embraces the mud wall
Laced with yellow pumpkin flowers.

Just off the wall I hear the sea
Call me aloud; I submerge under the sound,
Under the sound.

The moist wind blows cold,
Biting my flesh; all things
Taste bitter like so much black coffee.

I wish to return. How I remember the grove,
Hillocks, the creek in my home town!
Memories of childhood crowd upon me.
Would that the sea were Mother
So that I might find peace in her bosom;
I wish to rest peacefully
Under the downy swells.
The homesick silvers hazily over the sealine
In the distance.

Let me mend the ripped tent of memory
Sitting idly on the beach.

LAMB

The little lamb today again
Gazes at the far-off hill.
Over the fresh green timberline
Drift the clouds as if
Tiptoeing in the blue heaven.

The little lamb today as always
Listens to the birds far away,
Their hilarity of song sounds
In waves in the wind.

The little lamb today as usual
Gazes upon the passing clouds
Wondering if his mother will return
From across the hill crest.

The little lamb today like always
Listening to the birds,
Longs for the tender voice of his mother.

THE IMAGE OF RAIN

The sick sky splashes down cold rain.
The rain tears off the twigs of roses
And makes away with the lovely rainbow
In my heart.
Where has my Boyhood gone,
With its burden of sorrow?

Tonight
Rain beats upon the windowpanes
As if hammering down a nail
Into the coffin of my boyhood.

My heart, mourn your own death.
Go your lonely way
To the lonely grave by the sea.

Sŏ, Chŏngju (1915-)

Born in Kochang, North Chŏlla Province, Sŏ studied Buddhism at Hehwa Buddhist College. During the year 1936 he edited and published *Siinburak* (Poets' Village). *The Snake*, his first book of verse, came out in 1941. In 1940 he left for Manchuria where he had led a wanderer's life before he came back home on liberation in 1945. Sŏ's basic philosophy of art is rooted in aestheticism. His magic manipulation of language and his superb employment of the evocative power inherent in Korean sentiment make him the rarest talent in the whole gamut of modern Korean poetry. His work includes *The Snake* (1941), *The Nightingale* (1948), *Selected Poems of Sŏ Chŏngju* (1956), *The Notes on the Silla Dynasty* (1961), *The CompleteWorks of Sŏ Chŏngju and Myths in Chilmaje Village* (1975).

THE NIGHTINGALE

Tears glinting
When azaleas raindrop their petals
My love has gone away in a gentle tread
Playing on the flute a thousand miles to the West.

Adjusting her cotton dress again and again
My love has gone away a thousand miles to the West,
The journey of no return.
I should have woven for her a sad tale
Into a pair of fine hempen sandals
Or cut off with a silver knife
My useless hair to plait for her.

A paper lantern flickering,
Night sky sprawled, tired,
Its throat wet in the galaxy that curves
Across the heaven
The nightingale strains out a heart-rending song
As if drunk with its own blood.

O my love who has gone alone so far away
Beyond the rim of the sky!

BESIDE THE CHRYSANTHEMUM

For a chrysanthemum to bloom
The scops owl* must have been singing
Ever since springtime.

For a chrysanthemum to bloom
Thunder must have roared
And rumbled in the inky clouds.

How tenderly it reminds me of my sister
Who stands before her mirror
Now back from the alley of youth
Fevered with yearning and wistful desire.

For your golden petals to unfold
It frosted so hard last night;
I had to spend sleepless hours.

* Often the bird is mistakenly identified with the nightingale.

MIDDAY

Over the path between red flowers
Whose taste causes a drowsy death,

Over the tortuous ridge
Stretched limp as if drugged in opiate
My love runs away, calling me after.

I follow her, holding in both my hands
The pungent scented blood dripping from my nose.

In the scorching midday calm, hushed as night,
Our two bodies burn and glow.

FLOWER-GIFT

A good many years ago,
Seized by surging solitude
I wandered lonely
Into the countryside where
I carefully gathered wild flowers
Into a bouquet, which I handed
To a boy playing by the roadside.
That roadside boy
Must be grown up by now.
I wonder if he knows
How to give the flowers
He collected by way of
Relieving his loneliness.
Again some generations hence
Will a flower-gift pass round
To a boy in another time?
And then one day at dusk-fall
In a thousand years or more,
In a hollow of wilderness,
In an out-of-the-way spot
Somewhere on a rugged hill,
Will there be another wanderer,
A flower in hand, and
Another child waiting for the gift?

BLUE DAYS

Come dazzling blue days
We shall love those we love.
Look where autumn once blazed
The fatigued green into flames.
Who cares if it should snow now?
Who cares if spring comes around?

What if you alone should live and I die?
What if I alone should live and you die?

THE LEPER

Cursing in sorrow
The sun and the blue sky by day
The leper eats up a babe
In the moonswept barley field.
He weeps red tears all night through
Like flowers red.

LOOKING AT MT. MUDUNG*

Poverty is a mere label for rags and tatters
For it can hardly hide our natural skin and mind
Which are constant as the summer mountain
That discloses its emerald green ridges
In the dazzling sun.

As the green mountain secretly feeds
Orchids and exquisite herbs on its lap,
So we must bring up our young ones.
In the afternoon when worries weigh us down,
Dear married couples, take it easy
Now sitting together and then lying side by side;
Wife regarding her man in love,
Man caressing his woman on the forehead.

Even if dumped into the brambles or into the ditch,
We must go with the belief that we will endure
Like hidden jewels with green moss richly gathered.

* The name of a mountain some five miles east of Kwangju, the capital of South
Chŏlla Province.

THE WINTER SKY

I have rinsed
In the dream of millenial nights
The delicate eyebrows of my sweet love
Enshrined in the recess of my heart
And transplanted them in the heaven.
The most ferocious bird in mid-winter
Flies at a cautious distance from the eyebrows.

Kim, Chonghan (1916-1944)

Born in Myŏngchŏn, North Hamgyŏng Province, Kim graduated from the Fine Arts Department of Nihon University, Japan. As a boy he published a considerable number of folk songs. His recognition came through *The Literary Composition* in 1939. As a champion of purity of art he rejected the intrusion of any foreign elements into art such as political ideology or propaganda. His work includes *Like Apricot Blossoms* (1940), *In Praise of Mother*, n.d., in Japanese and *White Snow* (1943) in Japanese.

SCENERY AROUND AN OLD WELL

A weeping willow keeps sentry
Over an old well.
In this lunar month of April
A patch of blue sky floats on the water.
Hello, Auntie,
Can you tell me if that cuckoo
Is the same old one that caroled last year?

Quiet by nature she smiles so gentle
And scoops a dipperful of blue sky,
Scoops a dipperful of blue legend.

Now an ox returns home across the hill.
The blue sky brims over the water jug
Balanced on her head, my auntie.

POEM FOR OLD GARDEN

Night has sucked up the village.
The sound of frogs has swallowed the night.
Lanterns begin to sway one by one
In the chorus of frogs.

Soon the wan harvest moon
Slips out in sight to spew
A silvering landscape.

SONG FOR HOMELAND

The moon shines upon the Sungari.
So thoughtful of my solitude
The moon has followed me
Wherever I roam a thousand miles.
                    a thousand miles.

My homeland is so far away
My very thought can hardly
Cover the distance. O moon
Are you sent here by my love
                    by my love?

When snow drifts far at night
I can hardly overcome this sorrow
And I weep and weep through the night.
I am now twenty
I am twenty now.

Wherever you stay
There is a home in your heart.
But how can I defy this desire
Of mine to return to that old place
                    to that old place?

When it is autumn and
Wild geese wing heavenward
I see in my dream the boats
Ferrying across the Tumen River.

Park, Tujin (1916-   )

Born in Ansŏng, Kyŏnggi Province, Park published his first poems in 1939 in *Munjang* (Literary Composition). Like two other members of the Blue Deer Group, he seeks his material in physical nature: mountains, trees, the sea, the sun. He looks to nature for the salvation of corrupted humanity. His work includes *The Blue Deer Poems* (1946), in collaboration with Park Mog-wŏl and Cho Chi-hun, *The Sun* (1949), *Midday Prayer* (1953), *Selected Poems* (1956), *Alpine Plants* (1973), *Lives of Apostles* (1973) and *Biography of Stone and Water* (1976).

THE HYANGHYON RIDGE

Beyond the mountain thick with dwarf pines
around the base rises another massive mountain
folded into another, hardly visible that my mind
makes a steed of a passing cloud.

The towering mountain, the massive, prostrate
mountain where tall pines spread over every nook
of valleys. The wild fruit vine akin to wildgrape vine
and wild pear vines claw the rocks.

Among the oaks and rushes thickly growing, all kinds
of beasts and reptiles like badger, fox, deer, hare,
weasel, lizard, yellow snake are found
inhabiting the mountain and mountain.

Mountain, you may as well be bored in your silence
kept infinity of time.

Mountain, shall I wait for the flame to leap out
of your towering peaks and prostrate ridges alike?
Shall I wait for the days when the wild beasts like
foxes and wolves—now lost to carnage—leap in joy
with deer and hares in search of bush clovers
and arrowroots?

THE STARS

—Composed in the Diamond Mountains—

How I have come this far crossing hill after hill!
No signs of life, no birds, no beasts around
in the high noon, I have come this far
lost in thought through the valleys.

Through the bare albino birches, like the birches
swaying in the wind, hearing the sound of water,
rinsed like pebbles in the stream, I have come
this far so fast lost to loneliness.

The age-old trees, now decayed, stand
spreading their whitened limbs.

The peaks worn to a point whittled by storms
and snowdrifts soar in the sky, clouds drifting around.

Swishing, blows the wind muffled in the sound of water.

September. The tinted leaves drop to flow
on the green lake like so many petals falling.

In the dark blue night sky over the east coast
fishing village where I stayed the night before
A sea of stars studded, sparkling.

Now in my mountain hut open to the freezing wind;
in my sky that I watch
the stars again gather in gorgeous blossoms.

A HYMN TO THE GRAVEYARD

The round mounds of the dead in the graveyard
Seem not that lonesome after all, for they are
Richly covered with beautiful turf.

The whitened bones will shine in the darkness
Of the grave; the death smell will be fragrant.

The dead who fed on sorrow while alive
Will not be sad to be lying dead; they long only
For the bright sun that will shine someday into the grave.

Red pasqueflowers flame on the green turf;
Mountain birds warble in the air;
The dead lie silently in the grave,
Warmed in the spring sun.

EMBRACE

Though eyes meet eyes
            heart meets heart
            blood meets blood
            we remain strangers
            after all.

Though we often return to birth
                  return to childhood
                  return to cold habit
                  return to elementary vocabulary

And eyes meet eyes
      heart meets heart
      or mind meets mind
      we remain apathetic
      after all.

In terms of thoughts as they are called
In terms of living as it is called
In terms of ideals as they are called
In terms of what-not's as they are called
               as they are called

We remain apart
You and I in us
We remain strangers
After all.

I as I cannot be you for good
You as you cannot be I for good
When can it be
That I as the end of I
     I as my inner I
     I as my own source
     shall return from the remote desert
             from the remote solitude
             from remote tears?

Remote I by myself
Meet myself alone
Before my eternal return
To the oneness

There is death beyond where you are
And I abide in you alone
And I defeat solitude in you alone.

SONG OF STONE

I am stone,
the summit,
perched quiet all day
on the peak
that looks out
upon the sea

When was it I wonder
that the sea tossed me up
repeated to sit
on this vertex
and ran away
into the far distance?

The blue waters will not come
at my call, to my endless wavings of hand;
I only long, tilting my ears,
for the sound of the sea,
and stroke the far-off waves
only with my eyes

O stone,
when ever will you soar
into the sky as a blue bird?
When will the far-off blue
come down to soak through your being
so that you can flap your wings
to fly up into the air,
loosening a breath
of life

The moon and stars by night,
sunlight by day,
wind and rain,
and snowdrifts
have drained your blood;

your soul grows rigid
assailed by seeping hues
and dazzling colors

How could fair weather
last forever?
O summit
perched on this acme
looking out upon the sea,
you feed on heaven and sunshine
awaiting a remote day
when you can fly free as a blue bird.

BEFORE THY LOVE

Shall I sit face to face with thee, Rabboni,*
whose word sparkles flame into my eyes?
Will the bleeding wound on thy toes and palms and
heart heal this wound of mine, Rabboni, as I quietly
weep in the vale baptized with thy blood?
The mocking ululation of beasts turns into a song;
falling head over hills from a cliff, into a rhythmic motion.
If only I could swallow thy flame,
if only I could be whipped on the back by thee
the bitter tears would glisten iridescent like scales;
madness would become a rapturous rest.

* A Hebrew word meaning "a teacher" or "a master."

TOWARD THE BOSOM OF THE SUN

Behold the sun. Behold the sun blaze fire as it rises.
Let us walk on the fresh fragrant grass when the sun
rises over the hill. Let us take the dazzling path at
dawn toward the sun.

Be gone, Darkness. Be gone, Darkness that moans like
a beast. Be gone, like beasts, herding onto the cliff.
Onto the cliff, sunlight loaded on your back.

Behold those mountain flowers giving forth a pungent smell.
Behold those green leaves of trees fluttering as if
they dance. Listen to the melodies of birds, to the
song of the waters that meander through the valleys.
The sound that the whole mountain makes as it wakes
again to receive the light.

The grass sound the grass makes on its leaves.
The leaf sound the trees make on their leaves.
The fish sound the minnow-like silver fish make
As they mill around in schools in the clear water.
The stone sound the stones make as they are tossed down.

The measuring worms on the branches and the slugs on the
    bottom.
Cheered, I shout yahoy ho, baptized in the sun.

Low and faint but withering in unison rings the
singsong of all things green in the mountain
Of all living things in the mountain.

Mountain, green mountain with leaves of trees fluttering.

When the sun leaps and radiates
My ears open at your fresh sounds;

My eyes brighten at your fresh light.
Blood circulates afresh.

The whole body tingles as if to soar into the air.
I feel light as a bird,
As I walk onto the green morning road,
Walk toward the bosom of the newly rising sun.

THE SUN

Rise, fair sun. Rise
washed clean in your face.
Blaze and devour the darkness all night through
behind the hills before you glow coal red
in your boyish face.

I abhor the moonlight.
How I abhor the night when the moon shines
on the tearful valley and deserted garden.

Rise, fair sun. Rise.
I adore the verdant hills in your company;
I love to see them flapping their wings.
In the presence of the verdant hills.
I can hardly contain my joy, if left all alone.

I pursue a deer; I pursue him
onto the sunny hillside.
I will frolic with him if I meet him.
I will pursue a tiger, I will pursue a tiger
and play with him if I meet him.

Rise, fair sun. Rise.
When you rise, I will call aloud
for flowers and animals and birds
to gather around me
and I will live in peace and innocence as in a dream.

Park, Mogwŏl (1919-1978)

Born in Kyŏngju, South Kyŏngsang Province, Park published his first poems in 1939 in *Munjang* (Literary Composition). Like two other members of the Blue Deer Group, he also turned to nature for his material. His world, however, is set against the backdrop of local legends and foklore. Adept in manipulating language in a simple vernacular tone, he succeeded in fusing sense and sound. His books of poems include *The Blue Deer Poems* (1946), in collaboration with others, *The Mountain Peach Blossoms* (1954). *Orchids and Other Poems* (1959), *Sunny or Cloudy* (1964), *In the Darkened Window* (1969) and *Leaves Falling in Kyŏngsangdo* (1969).

THE TRAVELER

Crossing water on a ferry
onto the path through wheatfields

The traveler goes like the moon
in the clouds.

A single road threads to the south
three hundred leagues long.

The evening glow tints
each village where wine matures.

The traveler goes like the moon
in the clouds.

APRIL*

A solitary peak
where pine pollen drifts.

When an oriole complains
of the long April day

The ranger's sightless daughter
left alone in her lone hut

Presses her ear
against the doorpost.

* The original refers to the intercalary month of the lunar calendar.

BED-SHARING

I'll tenderly embrace you
in the bed, sheet uncrumpled,
mixing flesh with flesh.
I'll tenderly embrace you
in the sumptuous bed
rounded with a mist.
Mountain peak,
I'll embrace you, tenderly.
Sun and moon born
on the river coursing down
to soak all to the core.
I'll tenderly embrace you
in the bed
which has no east nor west,
and we'll return to you,
O all-soaking river!

LOVE

I am but a heart-broken dreamer,
a foolish dreamer.

There's a rock I grind in private
with tears that fall every night;
there's a rock I grind with tears
through the livelong night.

Whenever will my love and heaven
be mirrored in this dark
and impossible rock?

LOWERING THE COFFIN

The coffin was lowered
into the heart's depth
as if anchored by a rope.
Lord,
forgive him.
Placing a bible above his head
I said goodbye to him
and hastened down the hill,
my clothes covered with dust.

Since then
I have seen him in my dream;
his long-jawed face turned around
he called me
        "Brother!"
        "Yes," I responded with all my might;
he could not have heard me, though.
I alone hear his voice
from this world
where snow and rain fall.

Where have you gone,
my brother,
with your eyes, gentle, sad, and kind?
I hear your voice calling me
        "Brother!"
yet my voice cannot reach you now
from this world
where I hear fruit drop with a thud.

THE BLUE DEER

Against a hill far off
Rests Ch'ŏng-unsa Temple,
An aged tile-roof structure.

The hill is named Jahasan.

When spring snow melts
Over the twelve bends of the river
Where elms sprout young leaves and
Upon the bright eyes
Of the blue deer
A cloud floats.

THE MOUNTAIN PEACH BLOSSOMS

The hill,
Kugangsan hill
Is a purple stony hill.

The mountain peach blossoms
Flare up in one
Or two sprigs.

Spring snow melts
Into a jade flow of water
Where a deer,
A doe at that,
Washes her feet.

Cho, Chihun (1920-1968)

Born in Yŏng'yang, North Kyŏngsang Province, Cho graduated from Hehwa College (Sungkyunkwan University at present). He taught at Korea University and others. As one of the three of The Blue Deer school, Cho resorts to nature for the setting of his poetic world. His nature, however, is coated with the patina of history and polished with artifice. He goes into history and things Korean like old temples and costumes in order to discover beauty. Cho attaches more importance to form and structure.

His work includes *Mountain Rain* (1930), *The Blue Deer Poems* (1946), *Selected Poems of Cho Chihun* (1956), *Before History* (1959), *Lingering Tones* (1964) and *Poems After Blue Deer* (1968).

FALLING PETALS

If the petals are shed
should we blame the breeze?

The stars sparsely studded beyond the bamboo
screen fade out one by one.

After the nightingale's song
the distant hills seem to draw near.

Should we blow out the candle
now the petals are falling?

The falling petals cast their shadows
upon the garden.

And the white sliding door
glows incarnadine.

Lest the beautiful soul
living in seclusion

Be known to secular minds
I have some misgivings.

When the petals fall in the morning
I wish to cry my heart out.

TORIWŎN VILLAGE

Once over, the heart-rending war
strikes us less painful than a gusty storm:
Thatched houses lie gutted by fire;
huts caved in.

Sadness eating into my heart I walk
through the village razed to the ground.

Only a few soy jars stand
unharmed in heaven's grace.

I realize my own life has been guarded
the way the earthenwares remain unscathed.

Soon the scattered villagers
gather onto the ruined site;
they just gaze on the distant hills.

The sky spreads above the village
in the autumn sun

and those full-blown cosmoses
sway in the chill wind.

AN OLD TEMPLE

Goaded by drowsiness
while beating a wooden prayer bell

A handsome boy monk
has dropped off to sleep.

Buddha smiles,
Silent.

The road leads ten thousand *li* to the west.

Under the flaming evening glow
peony petals are falling.

GRASS NOTES

Down by the crumbled fortress a rock lies
worn out, slashed by winds and snows for ages.
Waving my hand into the distance I mutely mount
a hill over which clouds pass.
Watching a blade of grass washed clean in the wind
I feel my own body sway in the thread of air.

Would that we were reincarnated
into beauty of pristine life
to talk in a low laugh facing tired faces.
O stalk of soul that quietly flowers where the stream
of time flows in ripples.

THE PETALS ON THE SLEEVES

The sky spreads far out over the cold rocks
where wild birds moan.

Clouds drift over the river
seven hundred leagues long.

The traveler's long sleeves petal-stained,
the sunset tints a riverside hamlet
where wine matures.

When he sleeps this night away
flowers will wilt in the hamlet.

As if fevered with tenderness and regret
he goes in a quiet tremble under the moon.

AT TABUWON*

Finally I've come out safe from a month-long seige
to see Tabuwon dappled with thin autumn cloud.

Guns shrieking at each other
for a full month of offense and defense.

How close is Tabuwon to the city of Taegu,
I didn't know before.

To save a very small village
in a fold of free country

No single blade of grass
could meet its timely end.

Passengers, don't ask
for what is this mangled landscape
made a victim.

Head jerking into the air, the carcass of a battle
horse all limbs dismembered but head, its scream frozen.

Enemy soldiers fallen on the roadside
as if to sob in remorse.

Formerly these souls breathed alive
under the same skies

Now decay stinking of salted mackerel
in the chill autumn wind.

Unless fate-driven,
unless faith-led
What comfort for these pitiful deaths?

Survivor, I see Tabuwon one more time.
The living and the dead alike
possess no restful place; only the wind blows.

* A noted battle-ground during the Korean War.

THE NUN'S DANCE

Folded delicately into shape,
The fine gauze white cowl
Wavers gently.

The bluish head, shaved close,
Is veiled under the tenuous cowl.

The glow in the cheeks
Graces her in her sorrow.

The wax candle quietly burns in an empty hall
And the moon sinks into every paulownia leaf.

Her long sleeves against the vast heaven
Billow up as if on the wing.
O how shapely her white socks match her movement!

She raises her dark eyes to gaze
on a star in the far-off sky.

Her cheeks fair as peach blossoms
Are stained with a tear-drop or two.
In the face of worldly cares,
Her suffering shines like a star.

Her arms swaying and turning,
Folding and unfolding tell
Of her devout prayer at heart.

When the very crickets cry through the mid-night
The fine gauze white cowl wavers
Gently, delicately folded into shape.

MOONLIGHT SONG

A little knife sucks up the moon light. The moonlight smells
of ripening apples. The knife splits the apple. The moon rises
again from the very inside of the apple.

She sucks the moonstained apple. The girl is thinking of love.
She puts on a white night dress.

The moonlight comes down to sit on her breast.
The girl joins her hands. The moonlight strokes her.
She picks up a book of poems from her pillow to cover her
breast.

When she had eaten her apple, Eve covered her shame.
The fragrance of the ripening apple comes out of the book of
poems.

The moon opens the window and goes out.

The clock strikes two. Caught on the cross over the top
of a cathedral the moon is executed. The falling leaves rustle far
off. The girl's eyes are closed.

The moon, an eternal disc of light floating in the void is
her loved one's face becoming the moon and coming to life.
She thinks of the Venus whose arms are broken incapable of
covering her shame. She thinks of her man of old who left
without as much as touching her hair.

The moonlight slips into the girl's dreams.
Her heart has conceived the moon. The moonlight radiates
from her sleeping body. She prays even in her dreams.

Yun, Tongju (1917-1945)

Born in northern Kanto, a border area between Korea and China, Yun was brought up among Korean patriots-in-exile. He studied English at Rikkyo University in Japan after a brief stay in Yonsei University. Arrested by the Japanese police and put in jail on the charge of underground activities for Korean independence, he died in prison six months before the liberation. His works were published posthumously in 1950 under the title of *The Sky, The Wind, Stars and Poems.*

CONFESSIONS

My face that shows life
In the verdigrised copper mirror
Must, it seems, be a shameful relic
Of a lost kingdom.

Let me confess myself in a single sentence:
Is there any joy that has sustained my life
these twenty four years and one month?

Tomorrow or the day after in time of joy
I must write down another line of confessions:
Why should I have made such a shameful
confession in those youthful days?

Night after night I must polish my mirror
With bare hands and feet.
Then the mirror will show the back
Of a lonely man walking sadly
Under a blazing meteor.

COUNTING THE STARS AT NIGHT

Up in the sky where seasons pass
Autumn mellows in the air.
In this quietude
I could almost count those autumnal stars.
Yet I may not count them off lit one by one,
Because the dawn will soon break,
Because tomorrow night will be here,
Because my youth is not yet done.

One by Memory
Another by Love
Another by Loneliness
Another by Yearning
Another by Poetry
Another by Mother, O Mother.

Mother, let me call each star by name, lovely name,
Names of school children with whom I shared a desk,
Names of foreign girls Pae, Kyong, Ok,
Names of girls who have become mothers,
Names of my poverty-stricken neighbors,
Names of birds and beasts like dove, pup, rabbit,
donkey, deer,
Names of poets like Francis Jammes, Rainer Maria Rilke.

They are too far off
As the stars in the sky.

Mother, you are also far off
In the north.

Driven by yearning for what I know not
I write my name
On the starlit hillside
And cover it with earth,

Insects are crying all night
As if pitying my humble name.
When winter is gone and spring arrives
Grass will grow in splendor on the hillside
Where my name lies buried
As green turf breaks out on the graves.

THE PROLOGUE

For a life to be led until death
without a patch of shame;
under the scrutiny of heaven
I felt painfully hurt
by a single breath of wind
that stirs the leaves of grass.
I must love all things mortal
with a spirit to sing the stars;
I must follow the path
destined to me.
Again tonight
wind rustles against the stars.

THE CROSS

The sunlight that has been chasing me
now hangs on the cross
on the top of a church.

How could it have scaled
its steeple, so high?

No bell is ringing;
I fool around giving a whistle.

Were I to be allowed the cross
as was Jesus Christ,
who suffered but was happy,

I would gladly hang my head
and let my blood flow in quiet
like a flower flaring
under the darkening skies.

ANOTHER PRIMEVAL MORNING

Snow sheeting white,
I hear God's voice
Over the howling telegraph poles.

Any divine revelation?

When spring comes in time
I will commit a sin,
with my eyes wide open.

After Eve's trials of delivery
I will hide my shame with fig leaves
And sweat on my brow.

BOY

Here and there sad as tinted leaves autumn falls in drops.
Where leaves have severed spring promises to stay;
the sky hangs over the branches of the trees.
A mere glimpse into the skies paints the eyebrows blue.
The two hands are dyed blue too when the boy feels
his warm cheeks. He stares down at his own palms.
Clear streams run in the lines of his palms. In the
streams are reflected Sunhee's lovely face, love-sad.
The boy closes his eyes, tranced but the clear streams
keep flowing, Sunhee's eyes meeting his.

ANOTHER HOME

The night I returned home
My bones followed me to share my room for the night.
The darkness of the room is channeled to the universe
And wind blows down like a voice from heaven.

I look at my bones
Quietly bleaching in the dark
And I wonder what it is that weeps:
My self, my bones or my fair soul.

A loyal dog will go sleepless
Barking the night through.
The dog barking in the night
Must be chasing me out.

I must go away like a fugitive
Unseen by my own bones
To another beautiful home.

HOSPITAL

In the backyard of the hospital
A young woman lying flat on her back
Her face shaded under an apricot tree
Exposes her white legs to sun
Under her white gown.

Not a soul nor even a butterfly
Comes for her even at midday;
She suffers, they say, from chest-trouble.
No wind stirs the listless apricot.

After suffering long from God knows what
I have come to the hospital for the first time
In my life but my elderly doctor knows not
What his young patient suffers.
He says I am all right.
Despite the extreme trial, the extreme
Fatigue, I must not lose my temper.

The woman rises to her feet,
Adjusts her garment
And picks a marigold in the garden
To pin it on her breast
And disappears inside the hospital.

Wishing her well soon and myself too,
I lie down where she has just lain.

Park, Namsu (1918-)

Born in Pyong'yang, North Korea, Park studied law at Chuo University, Japan. Park started his career by publishing his poems in *The Literary Composition* in 1939. Unlike most of his contemporaries who choose to escape reality, Park clings to it. He believes in ideas in art. He theorizes that art is born only when ideas as substance are fused with artifice.

His work includes *Homesickness & a Tavern* (1937), *A Paper Lantern* (1940), *A Sketch of a Seagull* (1958), *The Garbage of God* (1964) and *The Secret Burial of Bird* (1970).

THE BIRDS

1
In the shoal of wind
churning up the skies
in the shade of trees
rustling in a whisper
sing the birds.
They do not know they sing.
They do not know they love.
A pair of birds, their bills
sunk in each other's plumes,
delight in the sharing of body heat.

2
The birds do sing
not for meaning
they do love
not for pretension.

3
The hunter aims with a load of lead
at the essence of birds but
what he gains by shooting is but
a fallen body smeared with blood.

THE CHRYSANTHEMUMS

1
The chrysanthemums madden the ground.
A providencemust have withered other flowers
Before the chrysanthemums culminate in grace
And fragrance in the clean, chill air.

Justly basking in the last glory of the season
The chrysanthemums unfurl exquisite petals,
trembling in the wind.

They burn their own frame
to intoxicate the world with perfume.
The chrysanthemums madden the ground.

2
The chrysanthemums are good for the palate.
Fry them to a crisp mixed with rice flour
and the petals taste savage.
We eat their tender meat.
The flavor cleanses our mind and head;
they bend their silver brightness
to meet our physical needs.

3
When planted in a pot, they tumble down
to the ground in a cataract of light.
Often they seem to shore up heaven
drinking up celestial dew.
Fallen amid the chrysanthemums
I turn into a chrysanthemum.
I sterilize my head that has been
polluted in the dust of life;
I fuse into the brightness of chrysanthemums.

The chrysanthemums madden the ground.

A TAVERN

A dog lying meekly on the dirt floor
blinks up at the counter.
A paper lantern swings all night.
Village drunkards rave at nightfall
in the main street
looking for trouble.
A painted waitress dashes out
to separate those frantically at grips.

By the time the counter is emptied
the poor village dreams
of feasting on broiled ribbed steaks.

HANDS (I)

We should not have parted that way.
I should have wailed or done something like that.
His hands held in mine,
Certainly I should have and so should he.

I did not, however, give my hands;
Neither could he.

How gracious it would have been
If only we had parted the other way!

He became more close a friend than before
yet he could not hold others by the hand.
As we were about to part I looked down at my shameful hands.

He had his own hands left in the battlefield
to save the fatherland.

He had no hands, no hands at all.

MIDDAY NAP

The deep green is rubbed
On the canvas into a gleaming mountain cabin.
The heat suffocating as if popped up from under the sea
Dozes in a midday sleep.
The hot sunshine, the sun's mirror.
Dangling on the bough of a tree
Wind sways the leaves.
Awake from the swaying green
A cicada sets about crying chee chee chee.
A female yawns off its nap mem-em-em.
The maturing time ripens to fullness
In a midday sleep.

HANDS (II)

The moment an object falls
The hand tilts up into the void.

How long has the hand
Possessed and lost?

How briefly it possesses
Volumes of emptiness!

When angry the hand
Turns into a shaking fist.

When the fist relents
It turns into prayer.

1940s and 1950s

Kim, Kyŏngnin (1918-   )

Born in Kyŏngsŏng, North Hamgyŏng Province, Kim tried his hand at writing while he was at high school in Japan. He had published his poems in Japanese magazines before he returned home to Korea after the liberation. A critic as well as a poet, Kim embraced the creed of the modernists declaring a break with romantic tradition. His poems appeal to the visual and cerebral aspect of language. His work includes *The New City and The Citizens' Chorus* (1949), a co-work and *Modern Temperature* (1957).

THE SUN PLUMMETS DOWN

The sun plummets down
To the streets in Seoul
Where sycamores green so thickly
That I fear they may dye my heart green.

What on earth did the army trucks
Ever bring to me, dashing madly
Over my lonely shadow?

Can you tell my past
When you run away like a fish
Darting out of the net?
Do you guarantee my future and my friends'?

Caught in the Moment
Which torments me with its
Shining image no more fresh

I slither into the boredom
Despite my afternoon conversation
With a university professor;
Logic grazes my skin like a breath of wind.

Unrecognized by shards of faces
Broken on the pavement,
Hardened to sorrow,
I turn a thinking leaf
Bleached like a handkerchief.

Then I turn the street corner
Where twilight towers
Like a telegraph pole.

Now I drink the green to the full
Like a sycamore.

LIKE A TYPEWRITER

Today as usual
I carry my youth aboard
An international train
Which rumbles fast away
Like an angry typewriter.

Setting purple affection adrift
I see on the streetside
My friends return dipped in the sun.
All the streets haunted by ancient tales
Brew anxiety and fear and formality.

Darkness shoots down on me
Like sunbursts as I leave
The sun and flowers behind.

Again in some remote days
When the parachuting affection
Pierces my heart,
O my love dear as mirror,
Bring here the transparent morning
On the wing of air.

WEATHERING

In the reality of life
Where we must live a day
Like a thousand years
Or a thousand years
Like a single day
With those we shall
Some day be drawn apart from.
What is the sense
Of swimming in the moonlight?
Or of strolling on the sands?

The only desire
With which I must go renewed
Revives me green at times.

When unexpected idleness
Cleans my musty thought white
I find your smile and seasoned lyrics
Held in your hand,
In the shade of time
Which sheds like petals.

Now brightens the path to the possible.

Hwang, Kŭmchan (1918-   )

Born in Sokch'o, Kangwŏn Province, Hwang was brought up in the north. Since he returned to the south in 1946, Hwang has been teaching school. Though he began his literary career in 1946, his major breakthrough came in 1952, when his poems were published in *Munye* (Literary Arts). His work includes Season's *Romance* (1959), *The Spot* (1965), *The May Mountain* (1969), *The River Han in the Afternoon* (1971), *Cloud and Rock* (1975), *A Little House on the Hill* (1984) and *Solitude, Nothingness, Love* (1986).

STAR AND FISH

Eyes opening at night.
The stars descend
On the lake.

Fish gape
To swallow them,
the miracle-beads
That impale the fish-belly
Only to float on the same old spot.

Star-eaten fish
Drunk with glory
Eye the clouds.

On a star-rising night
They alight
On the same old spot.

Every night eats up the stars.
Yet stars do not stay in the fish-belly
But float in the far-off skies.

SPRING FAMINE*

Down the pass of spring famine
a boy goes complaining.
In his tears mingle
the tears of his grandmother,
the tears of his grandfather;
his maternal grandmother is sobbing,
his parents streaming tears in company.

The boy remembers the tears
last shed by his younger brother,
now dead.

Mt. Everest towers in Asia,
Mont Blanc in Europe;
Huascran in South America;
Africa has Kilimanjaro.
They are all so far away
none of us has his bones
ever buried in any of the heights.

Yet Korea's pass of hunger pinch
gets steep in springtime;
many crossed it in tears,
many crossed pinched in hunger,
and some died while crossing.

Korea's ridge of spring famine
allotted for us to cross
towers 9,000 km high above sea level.

The boy lies buried under the green grass;
the skies are a mere grain of corn.
I can't see anything around.

* Now getting more prosperous every year, Korean peasants used to experience extreme economic deprivation in terms of hunger and starvation especially in spring time as recently as the early 1950s.

PRAYER

Lord God!
A tiny soul has just left
for your land,
the soul of my little daughter Aeri.

Long illness
has weakened her thin.
I fear if she could make
her long journey, safe.

Some may sin
out of luxury;
she has never sinned
even for fun.

My friends called her
an angel
on earth.

She's departed.
An eternal parting,
never to meet again on earth.

Lord God!
Leave me in your providence
so that I might see her again
in your land.

Lord God who loves
goodness in man,
Please love the little soul more.

MUSING

When I, discontented with myself,
whip my boy crying off to school,
The warbling of birds in the trees
Sounds as if he cries.

4 won for a pencil,
3 won for a copybook,
Unable to afford 4 won
Father turns into a paper tiger.

Years and years back
When I was a first grader
I often had to be forced back home
kicked out of the class
because I could not pay the 40-won tuition fee.
I think of my mother,
who wept silently to see
Her boy unwillingly back home.

On such a day
I am not pleasant
even when I come across good friends on the way.

No thought given to the pounding of ethics
I come back home to find my whipped boy asleep.
I hold his tiny hands in mine.
Fingers are dirt-grimy
under the nails.
Poverty-beaten,
Father turns into a paper tiger,
A paper tiger that wails over spring famine.

CANDLELIGHT

Candlelight.
No sooner has its wick
been ignited
it starts racing toward the end.

A fragile resistance
Against a surge of darkness.
From whom has it inherited
The spirit of silent sacrifice?

Fate, perhaps.
Unconscious of time-limit
The moment it's come into existence.

Though it keeps burning time-limited
It doesn't grieve
But relishes every bit of
The flowering moments
In a dance.

Han, Haun (1919-1975)

Born in Hamju, South Hamgyŏng, North Korea, Han graduated from Peking University, China. To his despair he found himself stricken with leprosy in his early twenties. He set about wandering into Manchuria. He came down to the south in 1948. Han succeeded in sublimating into art his personal misery and embittered life experience as a leper and outcast. Recovered, he worked with the Korean Hansen Association for the welfare of his unfortunate friend-patients. His work includes *Selected Poems of Han Ha-un* (1948), *Oaten Pipe* (1957), and *A Dirt Road* (1960).

OATEN PIPE

Fluting *fil niliri,*
I play on my oaten pipe
longing for the spring hills
and my old home.

Fluting *fil niliri,*
I play on my oaten pipe
yearning for the green flowering hills
and my childhood.

Fluting *fil niliri,*
I play on my oaten pipe
craving for the crowds of men
and human affairs.

Fluting *fil niliri,*
I play on my oaten pipe
wandering over valleys and crossing rivers;
weeping over hill after hill.

AMIDST THE PETALS

The cherry-blossoms blow;
The cherry-blossoms fade.
They drift and scatter like so many snow-flakes.

Amidst the petals.
On the petal-scattered road,
I return stepping on the petals.

The blossoms doze in the moonlight
As in a dream;
The stars and the blossoms
Stream amidst the blossoms
In the distant Milky Way.

The petals adrift
Beat against the leper
And nestle grieflessly
Into his bosom like a girl.

The petals are shed.
Shed are the petals.
Who has parted from love?
Who is leaving in secret tonight?

In the petal-shedding night
I retrace my steps into the past.
Through the petal-scattered road
I return
Stepping on the petals.

BLUE BIRD

When I shall die
And be no more
I will be
A blue bird

To fly freely
Into the blue sky and
Over the green fields;

To sing a blue song and
To cry
A blue cry.

LIFE

All that has gone
Is beauteous.

Here remain the disgrace,
The punishment and leprosy:
The skies I used to gaze upon
Stay blue as ever.

Torn between a flowering life
And a flowerless life
I stand crippled here.

Staying briefly
Under the eaves of a stranger's house
Weep
The disgrace, the punishment and the leprosy.

PUNISHMENT

You are guilty of being a leper.
This indeed is a ridiculous charge

specified in no article of law.
Yet, there's no defending my case.

It's been provided since antiquity
anyone guilty of a crime
is subject to punishment.

In spite of this, they've thrown
me out of the world of men

declaring me guilty of being a leper.
This indeed is a ridiculous charge.

Kim, Chongsam (1921-1984)

Born in Ünyul, Hwanghae Province, North Korea, Kim attended a high school in Japan. His literary career started with his association with other poets in the 1950s. His poems are characterized by his tragic vision on life, history and the age he lived in. His books are *The Trio Anthology: War and Music and Hope* (1950), in collaboration with two other poets. *Twelve Tone Sacle* (1969), *School for Poets* (1977), *A Boy Drummer* (1979), *Somebody Asked Me* (1982) and *Peacefully* (1984).

THE SALT SEA

I am as old and outworn as my shoes.
Someone has left his hut deserted,
whose roof is also old and outworn.
There is no drop of water there,
Only a nameless mountain peak
reflects the gleam of sunlight.
There's no single bird in sight,
The salt sea contains nothing in it,
no man, no trace of water.
No fork of a road of death, either.

WHEN THAT DAY COMES

I shall die sooner or later
in the mountains
or in highlands,
whatever the place.
I shall die
into a flute note by Mozart;
I am not cut out for this world,
I am ill.
I shall die soon
and be a spread of infinite plain,
a drifting cumulus,
or a boy that shepherds a flock of lambs.
I shall die soon.

A BIRD

Every day almost at the same hour
just one little bird was chirping
in the same old tree.

The same as the day before
thornbushes, three of them,
were aglow:

One was for Mother's grave;
another will take care
of a little brother's.

Every day almost at the same hour
just one little bird was chirping
in the same old tree.

Ku, Sang (1919-   )

Born in Wŏnsan in North Korea, Ku graduated from the Religion Department of Nihon University, Japan. He worked for daily newspapers. At present he teaches at Chung'ang University. In 1970 and 1986 he was invited by the East West Center to give lectures on Korean literature. He was awarded many prizes including the Seoul City Culture Prize (1957). His work includes *Condensed Perfume* (undated), *Kusang* (1951), *Poems of the Burnt Ground* (1956), *The Reality of Language* (1980), *The Crow* (1981) and *Selected Poems* (1984).

WAR POEMS 7

—THE GRAVEYARD FOR THE ENEMY—

O rows and rows of mounds for the dead!
They may not rest here in peace.

Until only yesterday we aimed our guns
At your lives and now with the same
Hands that pulled the trigger we have
Collected the torn flesh and broken bones
To bury in the sunny hillside
With turfs covered.

Death seems more generous
Than love and hate.

From where we are, your spirits and I,
Our hometown is not far—only
30 *li* beyond the boundary.

The desolation of this deserted ridge
Weighs me down like heaviness itself.

When alive you and I were bound by hate.
Now that you are dead your lingering regret
Is imbedded into my desire.

Up in the sky that seems to touch the earth
The clouds drift to the north.

Sporadic reports of guns far off.
I wail over the graveyard
Of love and hate.

WAR POEMS 1.

Out of the patched-glass window of boarded shacks
children's faces hang like a flaming sunflower.

The blinding sun beats upon them
to turn aside. I turn also.

The shadow about to wail follows me;
I stop by accident at a turning.

On the hedge in a heap of ashes
forsythias are about to open bud.

Chenny races down the hillslope
her front teeth all out.

I become jolly as if drunk;
shadow overtakes me with a smile.

WAR POEMS 2

Perhaps anyone could have been flung into fits of
laughter if he had run into a scene of a coal-black
octopus, smeared in its own ink, fondled and coaxed
on someone's lap.
As it was, sitting opposite I felt my face harden.
"Chongsik, don't be nasty. You'll get enough of sweets
when we get home to Dad's place." The pallid woman
appealed, by way of soothing, to her half-bred negro
child.
Well past mid-night aboard the train under the dim
lights, the other passengers, tired and way-worn, were
shooting unpleasant glares at the glistening heads of
the two seated across from me: the pale, sweat-stained
forehead of the tearful mother and the whining head
of her soot-black child.

Vexed at the sad situation, the unpleasant glares and
the pitiful figure of a woman with her black child
in her arms, I offered the child a pack of Haitai
drops from my pocket, which had been thrust into my hand
by a friend, a bit drunk, when he came to see me off
at the depot. As expected, the child snatched a piece
off in his black hand and chewed it in his mouth, his
eyes blinking dark as obsidian and then subsided into
silence.
Two, three, four . . . with each piece he inched toward me
until he stepped onto my laps grinning, his teeth marble
white. Now almost cornered I had to accept my fate; I
was trusted with the child from his mother while she
apologized with tears full in her eyes. I tried to
please him with all the tricks I had with the help
of the drops much as I would played with an ape in
the city zoo.

By now the situation was quite reversed. The tired woman who had been blankly staring at me, her savior so to speak, fell into a light sleep and the little savage quite satisfied fell to snoring in my arms. Unavoidably turned into his father, I closed my eyes full of emotion and a skein of thoughts.

Then I pictured in my mind: a few banknotes might have been the secret cause of this child's birth. I imagined the child's father, his body rolling dead somewhere on a Korean hillside or his beaming face as he proudly returned home with medals and decorations dangling from his breast.

I can read our own fate today in the face lines of the woman sleeping exhausted across from me. While I hold this young innocent life breathing gently asleep in my arms, I shudder at the futile destiny of man.

The train as before speeds through the darkness like a bullet. The passengers, all tired as rags, have fallen fast asleep, while I, with sweat forming into beads on my forehead, feel myself transformed into the black and white image of a father with his child in his arms.

WAR POEMS 3

Across the tundra of my heart
the nipping wind from Siberia sweeps.

Dry grass rolls tangled in windrows.
In a garbage pit lie jumbled the gaping cans,
bottomless ration-boxes, a ripped Star-and Stripes,
neckless bottles; in other corner lies a dead poodle,
bullet-hit; in the wake of a tank's caterpillar tread,
the carcass of a bone-dry cat. Way over, in front of a
tent as good as a vinyl-roofed green house, a G.I.
paces back and forth whistling inside the wire entangle-
ments draped by a blood-stained trousers. And then a batch of
gaudy-scarfed girls stick out their heads from the
pit-like houses like so many hylas from the trees.

Suddenly the sky froths black at the mouth.
A flock of crows climb up the air
to wing across the darkening mountains.

How my back itches!
How nausea chokes me!
Who is responsible for this?

THE RAVEN

1
croak croak croak croak
Hello, friends,
I cannot but feel a little sorry
for you
for I have an endless list
of songs to please you with
and yet this is the only melody
I can make:
croak croak croak croak

2
A raven croaks seated
in midroad of the expressway
down which a flighty bus speeds by on a spring picnic:
croak croak croak croak

Formerly, just one or two *croaks* I utter from a hill-top
tree were enough to make people stop, feel uneasy
about their behavior, examine their modes of living,
muse on death or at times reflect on eternity.
croak croak croak croak

What's become of today's world? Cars race along
bumper-to-bumper much less stop at me crying
desperately in the middle of the asphalt road;
glances thrown out the tight-shut car window
doubting if such worthless wildlife has been
kept alive.
croak croak croak croak
I cry to those humans who take for songs the silly
sound of sparrow driven out of the streets, of a caged
parakeet, of a cuckoo behind the chicken wire at the
zoo. To think what kind of world they are planning
for today and tomorrow!
croak croak croak croak

A raven croaks persistently sitting in midroad
of the expressway near Osan Interchange
as if determined to be run over dead.

SHAME

Ch'anggyŏngwŏn Zoo.
I peep across the wire netting
behind the iron fence;
I intently look for an animal
which possesses a sense of shame.

Hi, Manager, can you tell me
if there's any signs of it
on the flaming rear of a monkey?

On the bear's paw, unendingly licked by its owner?
On the otter's moustache?
Or on a female parakeet's beak?

I have come to the zoo
in search of a sense of shame
long since atrophied
in the city dwellers.

Yi, Tongju (1920-1979)

Born in Haenam, South Cholla Province, Yi attended Hehwa College which he left without earning a degree. His first poems were published in 1946 in *Munhak Yesul* (Literary Arts). Yi's poems successfully reveal the natural flow of the vernacular. His work includes *Your Friend* (1946), *Bridal Night* (1951) and *Gang-gang-su-wolei* (1959).

THE GREAT BUDDHA IMAGE

His smile radiates so familiar.

The sun rises in early dawn
more in ecstasy than in dreams.

The universe is a blank
you have left us on purpose.

The blue skies abiding so far
are smaller than your seating lotus leaf.

The smouldering rancor in hell
will melt as the spring snow.

Unendingly drained, your grace
still fills its vessel to the brim.
A midnight star beams on the quiet depth.

The sacred crane folding its wings,
clouds play meekly around your knees.

Your vessel overflows though it seems unfilled.

GANG-GANG-SUWOLEI*

Silver fish swarm into the rapids.
Petals strewn on the waters
whirl in a moon halo.

Gang-gang-suwolei,
We never sing but sorrow arises.

In a white rose garden
a peacock dozes under a spell.

Let us leap and leap around
waltzing to the chanting of gang-gang-suwolei.

Streaming ribbons wrap around the world;
long locks of hair entwine us all.

The moonlight is stronger
than wine when drenched in dew.

Flags are torn to pieces;
reeds are blown down flat.

Gang-gang-suwolei,
Gang-gang-suwolei.

* This is the chanted refrains of a circle folk dance. To reproduce the melody of
the original poem is practically impossible.

THE BRIDE

Her tongue tied tight,
the bride brightens into a flower releasing
her pent-up thoughts at her own parent's home.

Once back home to her in-laws
she metamorphoses into an obedient butterfly,
her lips sealed tight.

She bites her lips to wrap her tears
in the folds of her breast-tie.
Turning around in quietness she lets her laugh
slip across the back of her modest hand.

When someone hems into the house
she drags her long skirt in a hurry,
her hands folded in awe
and withdraws into her little shell;

She casts herself into a picture
framed half hidden at the door post.

She is a mother, kind and generous,
to a shrew-like sister of her husband.

Affection is bound by law;
she writes in a graceful court style
to her husband who never comes back to her.

The bride whose hair tidy as a quill
is now a mother, her silver hair let loose;
she can hardly thread a needle, her sight dimmed

Though her son is a floating cloud
She pins on him her mountain-like hope
and waits for dawn as calmly
as she awaits her own death.

Kim, Suyŏng (1921-1968)

Born in Seoul, Kim studied English at Yonsei University. His literary career started with *The New City and Citizens' Chorus*, a book of poems collected in collaboration with Pak Inhwan and Kim Kyŏngnin. Kim was strongly committed to the society of which he was a member. He has another book of poems, *The Game on the Moon* (1959).

SNOW*

Snow stirs with life.
Snow, fallen, stirs with life.
Fallen on the ground, snow stirs with life.
Let us hem**
Let us hem, young poets.
Let us hem to the snow.
Let us hem free and aloud
so that snow may heed us.

Snow stirs with life till long after dawn.
Snow stirs with life
for the spirit and body that are foreign to death.

Let us hem,
Let us hem, young poets,
In the sight of snow.
Let us cough out the phlegm
that's been deposited in the heart all night long.

* The pronunciation of the word 'snow' in the original may suggest three different meanings: *nun* as 'snow,' *nun* as 'sprout,' *nun* as 'eye.'
** The pronunciation of the original may also suggest 'rise' (ki'chim), besides a short cough made to gain attention.

A WATERFALL

It falls over the upright cliff
without a hint of fear.
A thing incapable of definition.
Without meaning to fall into any specific purpose
it falls incessantly like a noble spirit
day and night regardless of seasons.

When marigolds and houses fuse in the night darkness
it falls sounding upright sounds.

The upright sound sounds upright.
The upright sound summons another upright sound.

The water dropping like a bolt of lightning
afford not a moment of intoxication;
it falls without height or width
as if capsizing stupor and stability.

FOLDING SCREEN

Screen shuts me out from anything.
Face of renouncement.
Standing mindless like one drunk with death
screen concerns nothing at all.
In its face of death incarnate
dwell dragons and sunset.

Declaring a break with grief
screen studs a flying waterfall and a remote
islet on the height greater than that of falsity.
Placed in a most embarrassing site
screen wards off death by means of death.

I watch the screen;
the moon behind my back beams
on the red seal of its painter,
sixty-seven-year-old master.

WITH A FLY

To one sick as I
even the fly seems no more the same as yesterday.
Civilization without shedding its commonplace
plagues me again today as usual.

In the soughing of chill autumn wind
tradition alights like bird
in the shade of a tree.

The reason that I think of illness
the reason that I hang on to illness
is that I still enjoy my health
that I have great sorrow left in me
that I can afford something more
that I know how to meet death
calmly like the buzz of a fly
that streaks across the sunny wilderness.

GRASS

Grass lies flattened
leaning in the rain-driven east wind
grass lies flattened
until it weeps

Skies clouded, grass wept more
before it lay flattened again.

Grass lies flattened
lies flattened before the wind does
weeps before the wind does
rises before the wind does

Skies clouded, grass lies flattened
flattened
ankle-deep
flattened sole-deep
though it lies flattened after the wind
it rises before the wind does,
though it weeps after the wind
it smiles before the wind does,
skies clouded, grass roots lies flattened before anything.

Cho, Pyŏnghwa (1921-)

Born in Ansŏng, Kyŏnggi Province, Cho studied physics and chemistry at Tokyo Superior Normal School. Undoubtedly the most prolific writer yet known in Korea, Cho has more than 20 books of poems to his credit. Simply stated, his poems make vignettes of words on the everyday experiences of city life. His main theme is the lonely fate of man. Among his work are *An Undesirable Heritage* (1946), *One Day's Comfort* (1950), *Before Love Is Gone* (1955), *Night's Story* (1963), *In Search of Time's Lodging* (1964), *The Osan Interchange* (1971), *Between Dust and Wind* (1972) and *Mother* (1973).

THE SHORE

The sea
winter sea
raises a lonely shout
and recedes

All in all
driven by yearning
it comes back again
only to go back

Only a beacon on the sunset shoreline
beams its mute signal on and off
but there is no one to take
a message from the distant sea

The sea
winter sea
raises a lonely shout
and recedes

WHERE WE ARE ALONE

There is heaven
Where we are alone

There is earth
Where we are alone

There is Time
Where we are alone

There is infinite absence
When we step aside
Out of a turning

There is a voice
Where we are alone

There is no cause to be mean
To think that much
It is no use existing that way

There is the universe
Where we are alone

There are sun and moon
Where we are alone

EMPTY AS DEATH

Anything empty as death?
Anything futile as death?
Anything lonely as death?

Dismissing death when haughty as youth
Sentimental death transcended by youth
Stillness of death indifferent to youth

Now bobbing up and down before eyes
Hesitating
You and I
One leaving, the other left behind
At the point of parting

Listening to death
Looking death in the eyes
Looking at the neck of death

Anything weak as death?
Anything pitiful as death?
Anything silent as death?

NEVER TO MEET AGAIN

We are heading where there is no address
We are heading where there is no way
We are heading where there is no use for words
Cut off from ties to things of this world—
Tears, attachment, joy and suffering—
We are moving to where there is no address
Moving from this world visible
To that world invisible
Each one separately
From the other
Day in day out

MIGRATORY BIRD

The migratory bird is by nature forbidden attachments,
Long lost to sentimental brooding.
It adores yet resents the sun.
It has learned from infancy to treasure its wings and
eyes.
Flying high is not its pride
Flying far is not its desire
Flying when is its merit.

No moon
Nor sun
Nor flower of any kind
Exists for the bird.
Flying when it should
The migratory bird is forbidden restrictions.
It is made to inhabit the currents of air
Setting solitude adrift.

SHELL

Shell
on the beach
feels lonely.

When lonesome
sunk in an empty hope
shell longs for the deep sea.

The more sun and moon pass
the more intensely shell
dreams of the sea.

All day long
on the beach of the great ocean
shell feels lonely.

Kim, Ch'unsu (1922-)

Born in Ch'ungmu, South Kyŏngsang Province, Kim studied fine arts at Nihon University in Japan. He is a critic and college professor as well as a poet. His work includes *The Clouds and Roses* (1947), *The Death of a Girl in Budapest* (1959) and *Balladry and Other Poems* (1969).

THE DEATH OF A GIRL IN BUDAPEST

Winter was setting in across Eastern Europe,
ice filming over the Danube,
roadside trees starting to drop their dead at dusk
when suddenly half a dozen Russian bullets
knocked you down,
more wretched than a rat dead in a ditch.
At the moment
your bashed head bounced into the air
for 30 seconds.
From your neck where head had been
blood was gushing out to soak the pavement
so familiar to you when alive.
You're fourteen, as reported.
Over your death
not a single white dove flew;
Budapest's night could not weep
freely over your death.
Now freed at last through death
your soul would return to ride
the blue waves of the Danube,
way off from the watchful eyes
and weep aloud for those left behind you.
Is the Danube flowing quietly?
Does it run as sweetly as Johann Strauss' melodies?

Why is it that a 13-year-old Korean girl
should have died, so innocent,
on the mute sands of the River Han
that's not made famous in music
nor well marked on the world map?

Why should she have died, her hand
jerked into the hollow of the air,
with the devil laughing behind her back?
Why should she?
O girl in Budapest, what you've done
isn't done on your own, it seems,
for the death of a girl on the sands of the River Han
rends in bitterness the hearts of her people.

Will the wrathful river be flowing
for certain today and tomorrow
bringing tears to the eyes of the people?

When braves are gone and following two months of resistance
your brothers and uncle were brought to their knees
at the same gun that aimed at you
will that river of memory be flowing
ever and ever through the conscience of man?

In the days when feckless Peters
deny three times before cockcrow
why should that man crucified to death
bring to mind all memories
on this sleepless night?

I was 22, in college,
thrown into jail in Tokyo
charged with being a reactionary Korean.
One day
I heard a voice, a sickening voice,
issuing from my own throat.
"Mother, I wish to live."
The voice I had never heard before

seemed to come from somewhere far out;
it wasn't my voice, yet it was mine.
Then I battered my head against the concrete floor.
I could hardly resist wailing,
sorrow welling up within me.

Who could have made mockery of me?
Did my shame stem from my desire to live?
Did the death that Budapest girl had thrown herself into
sprout from the seeds of shame
sown in the hearts of those trembling before death?
The greening sprout does not spring
from the impersonal vegetation but
from the gushing blood of the girl
fallen in the fight for freedom.
The greening sprout shoots up in an image
that betrays our own cowardice;
it springs into blossom
through the nights, sleepless and anguished.
Man will fall but he will rise.
Man will fall again and again for ages
shuddering in the abyss of existence.
Man will continue to weep with the parents
who lost their daughter to the devil's bullets.

Winter was setting in across Eastern Europe,
ice filming over the Danube,
roadside trees starting to drop their dead at dusk,
when suddenly half a dozen Russian bullets
knocked you down,
more wretched than a rat dead in a ditch.

IN JUNE

When you arrange flowers in a vase
My dear, I wonder
if your eyes and cheeks flare up as much
as those flowers that brighten a little
space in the room. Do they?

Locked within the walls, behind the bars,
in death of darkness huddle
the peony
the rose
the Chinese rose
the marigold.
Among them the silver-haired maiden marguerite
smiles shyly.
When you arrange them all in a vase
My dear, I wonder
if you sense a breeze play around
your eyes and cheeks awhile,
as those flowers flare up a little space
in the room.

Is it a song made by a rustling
of a thousand leaves?
What a pity the stupid darkness
stands in the way!
Blood stops circulating;
people's eyes get petrified.

So cautious
they have needles grow
on their own bodies.

When you arrange flowers in a vase
My dear, I wonder
if those mackerel clouds way overhead
will come down fleece-softly
to rest in your eyes and cheeks.

FLOWER

It is nothing but a mere pose
before I name it.
When I call it by name
it comes to me and becomes a flower.
Would that someone called me by a name
that matches my color and odor;
I shall come to him and become a flower.
All of us desire to be something
meaningful to each other,
you to me, I to you.

Chŏng, Hanmo (1923-1991)

Born in Puyŏ, South Ch'ungchŏng Province, Chŏng belatedly enrolled at Seoul National University after years of engaging in literary activities. He had been teaching at his alma mater before he was appointed the director of Korean Culture and Arts Foundation. He began writing in the 1950's when *Hyondae Munhak* (Modern Literature) and *Munye* (Literary Arts) carried his poems. His work includes *Superfluity of Chaos* (1958), *Lyricism of Blank Space* (1959), *Baby's Room* (1970) and *Dawn* (1975).

WHO IS AWAKE?

Who is awake now?
Who is it that cries without tears
in the middle of the night?

The wind races
in the dark
through the dry branches of a tree,
a thin brass sound.

A star spangles clear in sight;
a star shivers in the wind.

Who is awake?
Who cries without tears
in the middle of winter night?

BIRD

O bird that flies about,
invisible,
far out
in the lavender of mist.

Washed in the sunlight,
golden wings in a glitter,
it glides across the sky.

Streaking
across the dark:
a clear sound of wind
vibrates my heart-strings.

A sudden awakening of dawn.
A bird that flies far out
in the lavender of morning mist,
glimmering in
and out of sight.

LATE AUTUMN

Sorrow is eternally
silent as stone

Under the blank sky
about to perish

a cock calmly
folds its feathers

Like birds nosing nestward
cheerless without flowers
people go homeward
cossetting their wind-swept hearts.

BUTTERFLY ON A JOURNEY

Baby sets out on its journey every night,
swaying the night darkness,
traversing the river of sleep
and the glittering plains of memory
and flying over the rolling sea of tomorrow
until it gets stuck
at a hell-black cliff,
a forbidden *cul-de-sac*,
Just to return frightened out of its wits.

Opening a black cover he enters
and meets a whirlpool of chaotic fumes of gunpowder;
war is forever on fire.
In the lavender veil of fog
The green river of terror never steps this far.
Love is a blue bird on the wing.
Meeting is untimely impatience.
Longing goes elusive even in a dream.

My Baby,
back from dream-road
how you come onto my arms to unfold your wings
soaked wet in dream dew.
Today, in what fierce valley
have you met a terrifying eagle
only to return frightened out of your wits?

SONG OF STONE

The waves dash without cessation
to discipline the shore
of burning desire

White hands ripple
on the keyboard

How the sea shudders
wreathed in a maelstrom!

A breathless hush.
At early awakening dawn
how you make love, waves,
enfolding me in your body heat
and dashes to pieces!

I open a mysterious gate
and enter a secret closet
where I lie in the arms of deep sleep;
a breathing gently races in my veins

until I turn petrified
in the form of a spirit
that sinks deep in the waters,
and in that rich depth
I grow into green-mossd silence.
How the song of the by-gone days
resounds quietly within!

PARTING

Now so beautiful
it sounds

high-pitched tone
of strings or wooden pipes

shrill voice of vocal exercise
a number of parting
that have fled in *tremolo*
bruises left in my heart

like ice cream flavor
taste of sorrow has tingled my veins

upon the blue surface
of a rolling ocean
white petals waver to drift
and our parting comes to an end

To end is to rest at ease
or to pray in quietude

Onto the burning lips
ripples the moon halo
as memory ripples in a ring

Light on the window
blowing of a whistle
a white snow road

Pain squeezing the heart may be
a life burning itself
or dimly written words
washed out by streaming tears
or lingering perfume

now from afar
shaking in the wavering wind
beyond your reach
beyond mine
like a star in the sky.

Kim, Kyudong (1923-   )

Born in Kyŏngsŏng, North Hamgyŏng Province, Kim graduated from Yonsei University School of Medicine. His first poem came out in *Yesul Chosŏn* (Arts Korea) in 1948. His work includes *Butterfly and Square* (1955), *The Myth of the Present* (1956), *Heroes in Death* (1977) and *Selected Poems* (1985).

A LETTER FROM THE NORTH

In a dream you came.
You, who had suddenly left home at twenty-three,
Came back a forty-seven-year-old traveler.
How I have been wishing to see you once in a lifetime!
Indeed you came. How I've been worried about you
Day in day out all these years!
You just cried, your face buried in my lap.
You cried and cried like a child,
Cried your heart out.
You came back home, dear, surviving
The passage of these many far off years.
And you said to me: "I'll never leave you, mother."
Your tearful eyes said it
Again and again.

AN ERA

A stone has dropped
from the sky
I hear the wind
that ran away to parry the fall
come to touch me
The majority of men who have rushed
out from heavy and murky mirror
are nowhere in sight
When it downs
pillars and walls
rubbing their eyes blurred
loath to see anything
come toward me
around the dismal forest;
set alight
the empty site
of the half-burnt heart
And death smell
closes in upon the heart
and flutters like a bird's wing
Now I come down on an escalator
to see a moon fallen on the water
shaking
An era's odd face
gets sunk in the water
Hand stuck frozen to metal
refused to come off

EVENING GLOW AND POETRY

The evening glow that comes by itself
and burns troubles me.
Clawing its breast bare
The evening glow comes by itself
And burns eyeing reproachfully.
In the glow is always heard
A thunderous voice for cheers;
Is reflected my sister's face, so distinct.
By this time
The evening glow gets excited enough
To daub its red paint all over;
to beat a drum, dancing like so many farmers.
A glass of water downed,
Today as usual I meet, empty-handed, my evening glow.
No one in the city watches the evening glow any more.

HOME

At hometown
there dwells no burning passion or the like.

The village sits rounded by the mountains
And grows aged with the mountains.

In the village a row of poplars
In a longing for the far-off sea
Flutters sobbing in the skies.

By day the cocks in the neighboring houses
flap their wings crying classic cries.

At home
There's no burning passion
awaiting.

Shin, Tongjip (1924-)

Born in Taegu, North Kyŏngsang Province, Shin graduated from Seoul National University. He has published 13 volumes of poems since his first book of poems came out in 1954. In 1956 he went abroad to the United States to study at Indiana University. Currently, he teaches at Kyemyong University in his hometown. Among his work are *Banishment of Lyricism* (1954), *Another Prologue* (1958), *Seething Vowels* (1965), *An Empty Cola Bottle* (1968), *The Man on Dawn* (1970), *Sending a Message* (1973), *Passengers* (1975) and *The Sea for Three Persons* (1979).

A SHOE

A scrap of iron jerks its arms upright
in the field where an odd shoe lies exhausted.
A cricket says Mass inside the shoe.
Its faint voice soon dies out and
the quiet soft-lands on the field awhile.
Grass blades swaying,
the shoe screams all of a sudden
in a voiceless shout.
Come and listen,
the shoe is calling its mate.
Don't be misled, anyway.
A worthless man's feet
are useless even after death.
Where is my mate gone?
The shoe is releasing nostalgia in a body.
The cricket resumes its prayer
in the dusk of autumn.

VERTIGO

How long can man stare
Into his own whirling center?
How can he endure the vertigo
The whirlpool engenders?
Eyes can no longer see anything
But a darkness of noon,
A sun-blazing night.

Has there been a native place
Found ever beautiful?
Like a departure
It becomes a fire dream easy to rot.
Putting desperate pressure
Upon the burnt-out eyes
Man tracks down his own burning scar.
Let those willing to go, be gone.
Yet who ever can endure
The whirling fire of nothingness?
Once drawn into it,
Who else can get out, unscathed,
Unless he turns into a falling firebird,
Unless he turns into a falling meteorite?

CACTUS

Beyond the roof
The evening glow tenderly plays the organ.

On the fringe of parting May
A cactus blooms white for a single day.

My eyes spin a little;
What is left in the eyesight
But the poor vestige of flowers?

On my way back I ran into Mr. Yi
And had a drink with him.

On the fringe of parting May
A cactus blooms white for a single day.

Unfilled pages with unfinished words
Are patiently waiting for me on the desk.

All things remain the same as the night before.
No miracle ever takes place;
Only I am a changed one.

In the palm of my hand circulate the streams
That differ from those for yesterday.

Wet with overnight dew
How tender the world has turned!
Baptized in the darkness
How our experience has deepened!

From the calendar on the wall
Today's face so strange
Flashes in a close-up.

A HANDSHAKE

So many men have
Died in so many ways.
Those left alive have
Lived in so many manners.
And they shake hands
With each other, speechbound,
The dead
And those left alive.

What sense is made today
Out of shaking hands?
One of my hands
Is rooted deep in the ground;
The other
Resists the density of space,
While the dead long for the days
When they were alive;
The living picture to themselves
The day when they will die.

LIFE

Is life tainted?
Turned almost earth-colored
Its wasted face wears a dead pan.

How I wished to live for good,
To live with you,
To live to be something more treasured than death!

A starlight that has lodged in my life,
Through the dark of billions
and billions of light years.

Still haunted by the memory of gunsmoke
we call out the last names,
The names warm as flesh

Let the living testify to the dead;
Let the dead indict the living.
Loneliness conditions life.

I stop to watch the long way I've come.
Over my shoulder in the distance
Perhaps wind ripples in joy.

A SORROW

Before a sorrow is born
It takes at least one hundred million years.

Before a sorrow mellows,
Mellows into a song
it takes at least one hundred million years.

Before a song degenerates,
Degenerates into sugared water
How long will it take?

Fossil can tell,
Lodged inside the rock fault of the Paleozoic era;
The stars glittering in the night sky
Can tell.

Hong, Yunsuk (1925-   )

Born in Chŏngju, North Pyŏng'an, Hong briefly attended the Teachers College,
Seoul National University. Currently she teaches at Sangmyŏng Womens College.
Her work includes *Poems on the Korea Dynasty* (1962), *A Wind Mill* (1963), *On
Ornament* (1963), *Daily Clock Sound* (1971), *Women's Park* and *How to Live*
(1983).

SUNBEAMS IN AN ALIEN LAND

In the village where I live
by the old fountainside
is an alien land
where my mother wandered when young

The sunflower-glittering hedge
the tile-roofed western style house
the hillock
and the wind laced with lovely butterfly ribbons

Often a rain-impregnated cloud
peeks silently into the window
of a lonely alien room in summer
There are cold footmarks of destiny
which passes ahead of us wherever we go

For the past twenty years
when I was a cloud on a summer's day
in an alien land where my mother
wandered when young
there scattered around the village entrance
cotton-sugar vendors
who melted sorrow into rainbow

Now winter its blade sharpened blue
razed the sunflower-glittering hedge,
the tile-roofed western style house
and the hillock
And then I have moved into the present village.

ON ORNAMENT

That a woman
begins to wear her ornaments
one by one
means she begins to shed dreams
one by one

A wistful concern
with which to shield with fingertips
the specks
where petals used to be.

Like Eve who covered
her shame with fig leaves
woman must make up with ornaments
for the loss of flowers.

Do any teenagers wear
on their supple fingers
one-carat diamond rings?
They are dream itself.

Where love is gone,
where friendship and little star-like dream
Go rusty like a summer lawn,
autumn blows down a leaf.

To ornament is
to call for nostalgia,
to grace the last season of the year.

To open the window through which
to learn the unpolluted loneliness
from the emerald blue,

Or it is just I that will not be lost,
or a wing on which are carried
the intense dreams of a woman.

FANTASY ON THE WEEDS

The weeds grown on the hill:
Unfailingly
Today as usual
Soft as fuzz beneath the ears
The glue-plant dreams.

The plantain,
The purslane,
The racambole,
The thistle,
The valerian,
The marsh plant,
The wormwood and
The spikenard.

I could not resist my tears:
The dreams of a 16-year-old
Flushed in the blue light;
The dreams of the remote days
Slumber there.

One day
A man and his fiancee
Crossed the sea
Leaving his home behind
Where an old woman
Became wilted like the waist
of a wild window-flower.
That was my mother.

Outside the bamboo-gate
The evening primrose
Flushed as a flower-lantern.

Coiling up the hedge
The pink morning glories
Were in bloom.

. . . And then
The stars gone out of sight,
The peal of laughter,
The thunder of applause.

Now the hill is empty;
The wind alone is there.

On the hill
The weeds thicken to today as usual.
On the wing of the wind
Blowing gentle as the days of old
An untamed pony brings
the old days back
Tinkling its bells
Around the hill.

SPRING FEVER

I am a sick man
gasping for breath
before a touch of wind or flower scent
Spring is like a wanton wife
giggling at the forsythia fence

Hair let loose
Hair shampooed clean
It dazzles like a young wife
who grows daily mature and desirable

Confined to bed the man gets thirsty.
His careless wife gone hiding
in the forsythia fence
sniggers for a whole day
and he turns yellow like jaundiced eyes
keeping on watching the yellow fence.

WHAT I CAN DO FOR THIS AUTUMN

What I can do for this autumn is
sit myself on my chair
listen to the wind
check the mail-box once or twice
and return inward to my own self
like turning to a corridor of
an emptied hospital

Some dries up the earth into a seed leaf
raises fires big and small
and dumps into a vacant lot
white bleached rotten bones of sun
I cannot lift a finger
Icannot stop a single leaf from falling
What I can do for this autumn is
sit myself on my chair
part from the noon sun
and quietly wait for the afternoon
and cordially meet the winter's visit

Park, Inhwan (1926-1956)

Born in Inje, Kangwon Province, Park briefly attended Pyongyang
Medical School before he associated himself with a group of poets such as Kim
Kirim and Kim Kwanggyun. Sensitive to the feel of the time he tried successfully
to incorporate it in the intellectual coordination of his language. His work in-
cludes *The New City and Citizens' Chorus* (1947), in collaboration with others,
and *Collected Poems* (1955).

BLACK RIVER

In the name of God
We were groping our way for the last journey.

One day
Our ears buffeted by the military chorus
Blaring in the railway station square
We sat aboard the train which was racing
Against the direction of those marching to death.

From the seat criss-crossed by the sweeping winds
Where tainted desires were exposed in the nude,
A peasant's son was carted into the jaws of death,
Into the land choked with detonations and gunsmoke.

The moon glares more dreary than quiet.
The citadel of freedom won through bloodshed

Beckoned to us waving in the distance,
Stranger to us retreating souls.

In the name of God
We see on the moon above
Black river flowing

THE WOODEN HORSE AND THE LADY

We talked over wine about the life of Virginia Woolf,
about the dress of a lady who has gone on a wooden horse.
The wooden horse has galloped into autumn,
its bell tinkling, leaving its owner behind.
Stars fall from the wine bottle
Sick at heart they brush against my breasts;
a girl I knew for a time grows up near the garden bush.
Literature and life go to seed.
Love's truth is forsaken in the shadow of love and loathing.
The lady on horseback is no more in sight

Time passes but returns.
Once across the confines of withering solitude
we must part now.
Hearing the bottle fall in the gust of wind
we must look into the eyes of the aged woman writer.
To the Lighthouse . . .
Though the beacon has gone out of the lighthouse
we must recollect the doleful sounds of the wooden horse
to keep pessimism reserved for the future.
Whether all is lost or dead
we must listen to the sad tale of Virginia Woolf,
gripping the dim consciousness that glimmers in the mind.
We must drink a glass of wine with our eyes open
like a snake that restores its youth
after passing between the two rocks.
Life is not lonely,
and commonplace as a magazine cover;
what fear obsesses us that we have to part?

The wooden horse is in the sky
its bell tinkling in our ears
while autumn wind moans
in my fallen bottle.

WHEN TIME PASSES

I have forgotten her name,
Her pupils and her lips
Lodged in my heart.

Wind blowing,
Rain falling,
I remember those nights
When street lamps
Cast their shadows.

Though love is gone
The days passed remain.

On a lakeside bench in summer
or in an autumn park
Leaves fall;
They fall to turn to earth.

Though our love is lost
Buried in the leaves,
Though I have forgotten her name
Her lips and her pupils
Remain lodged in my heart,
In my chilled heart.

WITHOUT TEARS

In the field bristling with weeds
A soldier lies.
The rose blooms in the clouds;
A pigeon sobs on the roof of the field-hospital.

Waiting for the solemn death to come
He hears the heavy tread of boots
Marching to the front.
Please shut the window.

Charges for the vantage points;
Jet-fighters, trench mortars and handgrenades.
It was raining when
He last called 'Mother.'

Bygone days are splendid as a picture-book,
Each page filled with a fairy tale.

With cheers no more heard,
Bandaged white
He lies dead in an unknown territory.

Without shedding a drop of tears
By the name of humanity
He has offered his blood and his youth
For the cause of freedom.

In the field bristling with weeds
No one comes.

BLACK GOD

Who is sobbing in the graveyard?
Who is coming out of the gutted building?
What is it that vanished like smoke in the sea?
What is dead in man?
What comes next to the year after it ends?
Where can I meet my friend lost in the war?
Give me death rather than grief.
Wrap the world in snow-storm so that
No flower might flare up where the buildings
And pale graveyard used to stand.

O Black God,
The grim memories of the day
Of the year
Of the war
Shall be your theme.

Kim, Jonggil (1926-   )

Born in Andong, North Kyŏngsang Province, Kim studied English literature at
Korea University where he teaches. In 1960 he went to Sheffield University in
England where he met William Empson. In 1978 he was awarded the Mogwŏl
Poetry Prize. As a critic he has critical essays collected in *Truth and Language*
(1973). His work includes *Christmas* (1969), *At Hahwe* (1979) and others.

COW

Your large eyes darken
with the sad sky

where I see my own image.

Tell me why foolishness
should be wisdom.

I have long formed a habit
the way you often shut your gentle eyes.

TAVERN AT SUNSET

The blazing sun at twilight
cools like heated iron.

Rain drips somewhere in the corner
of my desolate youth
at the sunset of my life.

My lips burning red like a coxcomb,
I empty cup after cup of ice-cold raw rice wine.

If all my youth prizes and seeks
should end in a mere cup of wine,

what else should I cling to,
fret about and regret?

Repeatedly shouting my own name,
I fling myself onto the street
In the dim afterglow of the sunset.

CHRISTMAS (1)

Like our hearts too calloused for tears
the skies promise no snow.

I stop in the darkening street
to search for the star in the east.

Bethlehem is far out of reach
though the same day comes every year.

Is it a braying of a way-worn mule
that I hear faintly ringing in my ears?

I have no gold, nor myrrh, nor
frankincense in my briefcase, though.

Seized by wanderlust, I wish to roam
far into the cold for a sign of the birth.

Would I care at all if my *Mary*
were clad in a simple dusty cotton?

A lantern-lit shack or a dingy waiting room
Is more civilized than the straw-covered stable.

This is an idle thought, I know.
But just in return for what I feel for the night
May downy flakes of snow fall to keep us warm.
May kindly snow shower down like white blossoms.

CHRISTMAS (2)

In the darkened room
Charcoal glowed red;
Grandmother, long widowed,
Was watching over a little life about to go.

Not long
Before father brought in medicine.

How brightened those red dogberries
That he had gathered amid snow-drifts!

A little beast I was
Rubbing my feverish forehead
Against the cold folds of my father's coat-end.

Now and then snow was pelting against the back door.
It might have been a Christmas eve.

Now I have already grown as old
As my father at that time.

Though Christmas is around the corner
Good old things are hardly to be seen in the city
Where the same old joyful snow falls.

Turning thirty, sad, I suddenly feel
the touch on my forehead of my father's coat-end
Perhaps because those bright dogberries
Must have melted in my blood and circulate in my organs.

A NOTE ON THE MEDITERRANEAN

Plastic bombs would explode on and off in Paris.
Early morning must meet the sea of Algiers by now.
Here yachts are rigging their sails up, gleaming.

War and peace sound so false—
Mountain ranges along the African coasts
Recline draped in sheets of summer haze.

A lighthouse on the shore of Tunisia
Where another battle is raging, it is rumored,
Blinds its beam on this particular night.

"Portuguese Man of War" is not to be feared,
For it is another name of the jellyfish the size of a straw-mat.
Again next day the sea was dissolving into jade green.

Kim, Namjo (1927-)

Born in Taegu, South Kyŏngsang, Kim started writing for a school paper while a
student at Seoul National University. It was not until the early 1950's that she
established herself as a poet. Currently, she teaches at Sungmyŏng Women's Uni-
versity. Her work includes *Life* (1952), *Tree and Wind* (1958), *A Flag in the Heart*
(1959), *Music from the Maple Grove* (1963), *TheWinter Sea* (1967), *Snowy Day*
(1970), *Love Script* (1974), *Accompanying* (1976) and *Selected Poems* (1984).

A FLAG IN THE HEART

My heart is a flag
that is hoisted unnoticed
in time and space invisible.

When gripped by madding fever
I light out onto the crossroad
that thickens with snow
the flag's quiet shade
veils the snow path as in a smoke.

Is my heart's flag
listening to snow music?

I only wish each sunset
would go without regrets
that pile up one by one like petals.

Is there a gold-hearted friend
like the stretch of silken sands
where grief grave as an imperial edict
has sunk?

My heart is a flag.
Now sobbing in quiet
it prays in time and space invisible.

TREES

Look
how the trees love each other
preparing for parting.
Leaves and branches of a tree
are getting married to each other.
Seeing them always lost in thought
I know they are in love
with each other.

Today
standing in the rain
they get laundered
from crown to toe
in a wash of tears.

It is so lovely to see
the leaves love the branches
and the branches the leaves.

Leaves and branches
both love the roots.
Watching the stars shower
down their jewels onto earth
night after night
I know of their love.

Look at the trees in love,
so pure, so immaculate.
Leaves will fall before long
and only branches will remain;
they know they will part
and they love deeply
as much as they know of parting.

THE WINTER SEA

I went out to the winter sea.
The strange birds I missed so much
were dead and gone.

I was in your thought
When the wind savagely howled
Enough to freeze the truthful oath tearfully made.

Fire of nothingness
Was blazing on the swells of waves.

Not long
Before I end my journey
with my prayer over
Let me possess a soul
Which will open a gate
into more passionate prayer.

Though not long
Before I end my journey,

I went out to the winter sea.
The waters of endurance
Raised a pillar from the deep.

MUSIC

Drowned in the perilous sea of music
I cry intoxicated with its withering spell.

All my life
The eternal cloud drifting in my skies
Has sunk in sorrow.

I have spun much poetry;
Not a piece could have
Worked out my salvation.

Man lives half his life
Consuming it in dizzying scepticism;
The other half is led
So vulnerable to suppuration.

Like trees bristling in harmony
In the snow piling woods,
Like the night of peace
Descending after sundown
I wish to be.

Truth is fear;
Falsity, shame.

I cry intoxicated with withering music
Because it is truth, nothing else.

SNOWFLAKES

Here in the bleak waste of convention,
In the village of sorrow plaining in the shade of trees
Shut off from starlight
Snow falls so white—brightening as if lighted.

Skin fair as white porcelain, so impeccable,
Next to God's fingerprints
The snowflakes pile up in crystal cold.

On this day
If I should ramble into a mountain valley
Where pines sough in the wind; stopping by a frozen well,
Could I meet the dear forgotten face
Coming to surface?

My lonely soul keeps wandering.
If only I could make it abiding as the deep-sea.
Currents under the dead-weight of the sea.
I should not have whipped afloat my grief
That has long rock-settled under the sea.
Shall I sprinkle my scalding tears
For the snowflakes to burst them
Into blossoms?

Moon, Tŏksu (1927-)

Born in Hamhan, South Kyŏngsang, Moon studied at Hong-Ik University and Korea University. His first poems came out in 1947, yet his recognition was established with his work being published in *Hyondae Munhak* (Modern Literature). Moon attempts to employ a surrealistic technique in his writing. As publisher of *Simunhak* (Poetry and Literature) and dean of a college he is active in literary activities. His work includes *Ecstasy* (1956), *Line & Space* (1966), *Domicile* (1968), a co-work, *An Eternal Flower Garden* (1976), *June for the Survived* (1982), *Spanning a Bridge* (1982) and *Selected Poems* (1983).

THAT SOUND

That sound is a fusillade
Of shouting cliffs
That girdle the horizon in the distance.

It is the sound of doors
Slamming shut by the thousands.

Who has driven me here?

That sound is a laughter
From the murderous flowers in the wilderness.

It is a sneer of the sunflower
That gnashes its teeth over the fence.

It is a rhythm of feast that ripens
Behind the wall of betrayal.

Who has driven me here?

That sound is a thud of black
Blood clots dripping from the floundering heaven.

It is the sound from the alley of intrigue
In which blue blades of swords tangle like jungles.
Who has driven me here?

STAIRCASE

The stones tumbling down the staircase
scream awhile in savage pain
before they stop quiet as if sunk deep into water.
The stones tumbling down the staircase
spread far and wide like lush boughs
and glitter at times as a sharp-cut ruby
their murderous edge set in the moon.
From where the tumbling ends
a man walks up the staircase, step by step.
His feet hurt and bruised, scraped and beaten,
he drops flat with a heap of stones held in his arms
as if they were a bunch of flowers.
But he rises to his feet time and again
until he starts up, turned to stone.

OMEN

Over the valleys
spans a rope like a suspension bridge
on which pass by
hares, apes and wolves.
Snakes lie limp in a circle
biting each other's tail.
At present a section of the world
may go half-crumbling.
Between lands
spans a rope like a suspension bridge.
At midnight when people have gone to sleep
the sea slants down in mighty shoals.

ODE TO FALLEN LEAVES

A leaf unhooked from the branch
descends gropingly as if to scratch the air,
a pain of parting from attachment,

In a rehearsing gesture
of the all of earthly trials:
tumbling into a ravine,
sleighing down a hillslope,
rolling across a plain.

A leaf unhooked from the branch
comes to a stand, breathless,
on the cold asphalt pavement
in a posture of listening
for on-coming footfalls and their destruction.

A dead leaf intrudes, butterfly-soft,
into the room through a gaped window;
then descends unendingly
into a loved one's soul
in a gesture of replanting the springtime.

SIGNPOST

A piece of straw floating adrift
Is caught on a sign post
At the bottom of dead shallows
And is given a breath of life.

As he tears the air quick as lightning
An angel's raiment is ripped on the edge;
It flutters like a flag
Only to change into a bird
Which soars into the sky.

Is it a signal sent down from God far off
On this particular night?

Threads of light
Caught on a sign post
Flutter like a golden butterfly
The size of heaven.

MY AUTUMN

A ginkgo leaf like an angel's palm
slaps a girl in the face and feels down her waist.
A red leaf ventures down a 31 storied building
pacing step by step down the staircase.
Baked summer-long the sky is now a celadon porcelain.
Clouds spread out scudding in arabesque.
An Italian poplar, its slick lower part stripped naked,
is capped with a cascade of golden light;
it feels cold in a glistening of light,
My wisdom unable to ripen a single persimmon,
my love, to gather a single chestnut,
how much more should I go falling this autumn,
treading on a soul that moans in a metallic sound?

Chŏn, Ponggŏn (1928-   )

Born in Anju, South Pyŏng'an, North Korea, Chŏn came to the south right after the end of World War II. He won recognition with his poems published in *Literary Arts*. Along with Kim Kwang-nim, Chŏn attempts to fuse lyricism into intellectuality. Currently he is editor of *Poetry Literature*. He was awarded the Korean Poets Association Prize (1959). His work includes *War, Music And Hope* (1957), *Repetition for Love* (1959), *In Search of Poetry* (1962), *Lovesong of Ch'unhyang* (1966) and *Inner Sea* (1970).

LYRICISM

It was raining.
Trapped in the tree
The wind tore itself apart
In the rain.

You were clinging to my arm.
It was raining in an alley
That was anchored in the night.

In the swelling darkness of night
Covering my face with your hands
You questioned me

In a soft voice,
In a feverish voice.

THE PIANO

From the fingertips of a lady
sitting down to the piano
bounce
the live fish
unendingly
in tens
or
in twenties
on the tail
of flipping light.

I go out to the sea
to fetch in excitement
a sharpened knife edge
of the waves.

INNER SEA

I have a memory of sand.
Memory of sand, a woman's wet feet.
Memory of sand, a woman shaking water from herself.
Memory of sand, a woman stretching out her hands.
Ten fingers soaked in the sea and the sun,
Keep stretching. A woman is sucking wind into
Her whole body when the sun breaks against
The tassels of hair streaming down her neck and breasts.
Sun dust rises when she brushes her hair.
Memory of sand, a woman stretching herself,
I have a memory of sand.

MISCHIEF

I aim at a tree with a rifle.
I aim at a leaf on a tree-top.
Tired of the job
I suddenly hoist the muzzle up into the air
with the butt rubbing against my cheek.
The sky comes within the range of gunsight.
The sky grows big in the sight of an M-1.
The sky grows small in the sight of an M-1.
Under the sky I stand.
I look at the sky.
The small sky hurts my eyes.
The gunsight goes dim.
I quit my game.

Kim, Kwangnim (1929-   )

Born in Wŏnsan, South Hamgyŏng Province, North Korea, Kim began to write, in
his own words, a semblance of poems since 1947. He was editor of *Modern
Poetics* and *Vowels*. He attaches importance to employing imagery as an essence
of a poem. His work includes *Wounded Graft* (1959), *Bright Shadow of Image*
(1962), *Casting a Net in the Morning* (1965), *The Fall of a Crane* (1971), *Twisted
Vines* (1973), *A Mid-winter Walk* (1976), and *Heavenly Flower* (1985).

CONFLICT

I take out for a change
My wife who has foundered in the heaps of debt.
We get onto a *de-luxe* highway bus
Heading for a watering place.

I watch her for the first time
In eighteen years.
How thin she looks!
All these years
She has been hanging our children
On twisted vines
Like wistaria blossoms,
For that is what she is—so skinny.

Her hands and feet have twisted like vines
Around her heart which gets more entangled
Against its wish to be drawn apart.

How could have our ties been!

Look in the sky
Lest your labor be futile.

Why did you come into the world?
"To pay back my debts."

LANDSCAPE (A)

The crane lifts up
Thousands of broken
Iron fists of Cassius Clay's.

Rattling in a shake,
Gesturing like a bum
Without a cough
It rams down the hungry wall;
It flesh-bombs a Giant Tiger tank
That charges in a sweep.
Intestinal chain binding me is cut off.
And the hammer detached from the crane
Dashes out of reality.
A bird flies off
In a parabola.

LORD'S DAY

A brood of fledgling swallows
Was craving for food in yellow chorus;
the choir boys are glistening
olive leaves tilting heavenward.

The pipe organ was parched
with thirst and I stepped down
on its glittering scales
toward a shaded monastery

Where some altar boys, red bands
around their necks,
would visit three times a day,
candlestick in hand,

They would make a light in heaven.

THE BIRD

I aimed at a bird,
breath held.
While I held my breath
a fierce animal
shot a glaring look at me,
glittering like savage spear-tips.
From a branch stretched taut,
from a pristine branch
a last leaf unhooked itself.
Space burst open.
The moment
death is freed from the whirlpool of death
a bird of nature sings
perched on the muzzle of a rifle.

VACANT SITE

One day from somewhere a man came carrying his own frame.
He apparently was going to make a bonfire of his rags.

He squatted calmly like a beast forgetful of howling.

It was snowing all night long.
Children trooped into the spot to throw snowballs at him.
But he had already been released from the animal-like posture.

Again silence settled on the trampled vacant spot.
Remnant of half-burned straws fitfully trembled.

I saw smoke rising from a crematory.

Yi, Hyŏnggi (1933-)

Born in Chinju, South Kyŏngsang Province, Yi studied Buddhism at Dongguk University. His recognition as a poet came in 1949 while he was still a high school student. A fine critic as well as a poet, he works for a newspaper as an editorial writer. His work includes *The Bleak Land* (1963), *Poems for a Stone Pillow* (1973) and *Drought in a Dream* (1975).

A SKETCH

Each time I visit the mountains
I see autumn stripping another layer of her garment.
Untouched by desire, her well-developed body
is well matched by its bouncing curvature.
Her blue eyes washed clean and
her sweet perfume feast the senses.
Before this perfect beauty all other adornments
are mere rags, like driven leaves.
Every year I fail to catch her in the nude.
No eager eyes can ever reach beyond her slip,
for winter pounces upon her the moment she is
about to go naked; the rogue could not
have waited long enough. And again he must be
hiding somewhere in the bushes for any chance.

NIGHTINGALE

Man passes away;
The ruined castle remains.
How life's vanity stabs my heart!

On the crumbled stones
Moss has gathered
Like a sad tale told by time.

When the ruins pass away with time
The evening glow alone will flame
Under the hollow skies.

BREACH OF PROMISE

1
Promise resounds when broken
rather than kept.
Promise slipped out of mind,
Promise remembered suddenly but too late,
And therefore, causing tongue-clicking.
Somehow we regret, somehow we miss
And somehow . . .
And therefore we click our tongues.
Somehow it resounds.

2
The after-school bell
Rings in my ears when I return home late
Because I had to clean the classroom
By way of punishment.
The six strokes of a clock,
When I missed the six o'clock date with my girl,
The sound of destiny beyond my control,
Breach of promise makes destiny resound.

3
She is gone
Taking me unawares.
Parting over
I measure the depth of love.
As shade awakens to light
Breach of promise awakens us
To the weight of promise,
To the weight of life.
Somehow we reconcile.
Somehow we regret,
Somehow it resounds.

FALLEN PETALS

It's beautiful to see one
sensible enough to go
when it is time to go

Passing through the inferno
of springtime passion
my love is fading now

Petals thickly falling
we must go now
loaded with parting bliss

Toward the lush green shade
toward autumn about to bear fruit
my youth fades like a flower

Let us part
our delicate hands waving
when petals start to drift to the ground

My love, farewell,
you're my soul's sad eyes that mature
like water filling up a well.

CRICKET SONG

Cricket ripples sorrow
In the autumn night
Like a stream.

On the thatched roof,
On the paper-ripped window,
On the eyelids of one quietly asleep,
An old tale slumbers,
Time coiled like annual rings.

The moon shining bright
Prompts my tears.

This autumn night
All that has passed
Come back to life, remembered
And a cricket . . .

O
A piece of masterpiece!

Ch'ŏn, Sangbyŏng (1930-1993)

Born in Ch'ang'wŏn, South Kyŏngsang Province, Ch'ŏn went to Seoul National University for a short period. His literary career started with his first poems being published in *Munye* (Literary Arts) in 1952. He has three books of poems to his credit: *Bird* (1971), *At Tavern* (1972) and *Ch'ŏn Sangbyŏng Is a Born Poet* (1973).

RETURN TO HEAVEN

I shall return to heaven
hand in hand with the dew
that distills in the dawning light.

I shall return to heaven
in company with the flush of sunset
when cloud beckons while I stroll on the shore.

I shall return to heaven
the day when my beautiful earthly trip ends.
In heaven I will tell all was so lovely on earth.

NAMELESSNESS

The sunset so beautiful
beyond expression
was fading out

In the presence of this moment
and the oncoming night
I was thinking of tomorrow

Spring is over.
Yesterday and this very moment today
are blazing—O the burning sunset about to fade!

Why I have to cut a slice
from the far-away sky and etch my namelessness
without a day's delay

I wish to know,
I wish to know.

BIRD

Flitting onto the vacant site in my soul
that has lived alone and will live forlorn
a bird sings with flowerbuds unfolding
the day I die
or the day after.

When a song is sung loudest
for the joy of living,
for things of beauty,
or for love,
I am a lonely bird
left in the ditch or sitting on a branch of a tree.

Seasons of tenderness,
weeks of sorrow and joy.
O bird,
sing aloud your age-old notes,
known, unknown or forgotten.

The bird cries
as if to say
that he has seen better days
and had bad luck too.

LETTER

Now my belly is full, treated to a lunch,
I write to myself that has been starving.

You are not overly depressed, are you?
You are used to going hungry, aren't you?

Remember that there were times
when you lived like a lord.

I've been living these twenty years
counting on tomorrow.

And I write
to you, myself
lest I forget
I am full now.

Park, Chaesam (1933-   )

Born in Tokyo, Japan, Park left Korea University without a degree. He established himself as a promising poet with his poems first published in *Hyondae Munhak* (Modern Literature) in 1955. His peculiar lyric style is in the age-old tradition of Korean poetry. His work includes *Ch'unhyang's Mind* (1961), *In the Sunlight* (1970) and *A Thousand Year-old Wind* (1975).

A LANDSCAPE

As wind scuds across the grass
so the sun ricochets on the southern waves.

Soon
a seagull or two fly casually about
over the sailboats
that drift in flashing dots
as if bound for a distand land.

How my heart aches
to see those sails gleaming white;
how far will they go
before they turn back, so tired?

Is the wind to shelter in the shade of flowers
that are about to wilt?
Or the sun to shelter in the wings
of those birds or beneath those sails?

Tell me, folks,
this world and the next
part company.

As wind scuds across the grass
so the sun ricochets on the southern waves.

THE FLOWER TREE

As long as I believe in life
That a few, if not more, will lament my death,
Those few can be the glory
In the garden of my heart.

On the fringe of this flower garden
My heart trembles like the flowers.

Again
So many strangers after my death
May turn into as many leaves.

And my heart will tenderly rub
Its cheeks against the leaves.

Is it not so?

OUR MIND

The sunshowers prompt our tears.
Our mind resembles the sky spread over our country.
That is what we really are.

Like the clouds floating in the sky
Our mind is free from need or greed.
That is what we really are.

Nevertheless, my beloved,
In the back of our mind
The clouds cast their shadows in an alley
While the sun shines upon a stone wall

What shall we care?
As we go along with life
So much we lose and lose.
That is what we really are.

Is it not?

FLUTE HOLES

The sunshine, it seems,
amuses itself most
with leaves and waters.
So does the moonshine, it seems.
In a care-coated world
Can I claim remotest kinship to them?
Torn between solicitous parents and serving brothers;
Molded into a tainted pattern;
Turned into flute holes carved in my flesh
I weep like a submerged tree
I weep like a foot-soaking river.

A DITTY

Shall I go abroad to a far-off land
and live there a life of hunger
humming songs to myself?

When met with humiliation
shall I suffer there
more bitterly than in this land?

Like weeds in the crevices of a mud wall
Left standing in the back alley of my home town
shall I live a life—born against my wishes—
in danger of being cut short
any minute?

WOODS

Some seventy leagues off
My beloved is coming this way
some sixty leagues.

Nothing stirs
But sound of breath.

My yearning heart is
about to go emptied;
Her dark hair
begins to emerge in tassels.

Close to her sparkling breath
My own blurs my sight.

My beloved
stands in heaven
radiating glittering gold.

Park, Hijin (1931-   )

Born in Yŏnchŏn, Kyŏnggi Province, Park graduated from Korea University where he majored in English literature. A series of poems including "Ode to Merciful Bodhisattva" which was published in 1956 established him as a poet. He has eight volumes of poems to his credit including *Chamber Music* (1960), *The Bronze Age* (1965), *Smiling Silence* (1970), *Between Light and Darkness* (1976), *134 Four-line Poems* (1982), *The Stream in the Heart* (1982), *In Iowa in a Dream* (1985) and *Lovers in Lilacs* (1985).

SONG FOR EMPTY CUP

A single woman
sent a single man
a wine cup of plain white porcelain

The man washes his hands
and sits quietly;
Instantly he touches
its soft skin

The air brimming the empty
wine cup
dissolves of itself
into beautiful wine
Too late he nods realizing
that it was no empty cup
that she had sent him

LOVE SONG

I wish to settle deep in you
like heaven sunk in the pondwater.

Eyes flowing into eyes, flesh into flesh,
our lives are both on fire.

Though I am left all alone,
you share my breath, racing in my blood.

O flower that blooms in soul's darkness,
in one with me, and yet a distant island.

ODE TO MERCIFUL BODHISATTVA

Standing on lotus blossoms
that will never fade
for they are carved in stone
thou reignest timeless
over the finite of this world
so near us
yet at a far distance.

Which sea waves
can ever roll in to wash
the tip of thy feet?
Which winds
can ever rustle
against thy garment, light as air?

Thine eyes slightly closed
are forever about to open, bright;
thy smile faintly playing on the lips closed
will never fade
for it is part of eternity.
Thy mind brightening like the sun,
thy person suffused with flower scent,
thou quietly listenest in that mirror
held up to thine ever-shining soul
to the procession of innumerable stars

Thou holdest in thy hand
a dream-flow stirring of beads,
no finger stirring a breath.
Thy presence leaves me speechless;
Beauty drives man to despair.
And like a man waiting in peace
for his death
I have only to draw sighs.
Merciful Bodhisattva,
When I look at thee at this distance
I can hardly think about the touch
of a master artist

but I have only one wish to make in earnest,
though it is a foolish one:
May I write one single poem
to remember thee by,
the most beautiful poem ever written,
so that each word and phrase
radiate with thy consummate virtue,
thy calm, thy peace, and thy beauty.
I wish to write such a poem
too exquisite to call my own.

POEM FOR THE GREEN

On the grass stand
a horse
and two children
one holding it by the ear
the other by the mane
to water it
in silence

An artist
has drawn it on a wide canvas,
which fills with green only
and yet a close look
detects a horse smell
in the deeper shade of green;
a smell of the children's flushed cheeks
in the lighter shade
and even a smell of water,
unmistakable.

PINE TREE ON EARTH

From where a pine tree on earth spreads up heavenward
and a pine in heaven spreads down earthward
to become one hugging each other floats a subtle
Scent, rings a mysterious sound.

From water on earth flows up heavenward
and water in heaven flows down earthward
to become one, hugging each other forms
a rainbow, rainbow of infinity.

From where a wind on earth blows up heavenward
and a wind in heaven blows down earthward
to become one, hugging each other burns the sun
glaringly, washed clean.

Park, Sŏng'yong (1934-   )

Born in Hae-nam, South Chŏlla, Park attended Chung'ang University. Currently he works with the Seoul Daily Newspaper. According to Pak Namsu, he is in the main lyric tradition of Korean poetry typical of Sowol, coated with the feel of his own times. He was awarded the Modern Literature Young Writer's Prize (1965). His work includes *Things Lost in Autumn* (1969), and *Spring, Summer, Autumn & Winter* (1970).

THE POPPY*

Ready to faint when held;
to crumble when hugged,
that flower is no other than
the poppy whose fume once drowsed
the whole of the Middle Kingdom.
Though a mere yearly plant
it flares up my sunset garden
with its charm and beauty.

Eyes closed,
I see Emperor Shien of the T'ang dynasty
dance, King Sou dance, gone mad,
and Yanggueyfei dance
in the nude.

Ready to snap when shaken,
more enchanting when pressed by lips,
the voluptuous beauty
of that poppy, a yearly plant,
once drowsed the whole of the Middle Kingdom.

Eyes closed,
I see them dance;
a throng of nudes
dance around it;
dance drunk with dancing.

* Named after Yanggueyfei, it refers to the episode of her reigning beauty which captivated Emperor Shien and brought him to ruin in the end.

A WINDY DAY

Why is the wind
Stirring so ceaselessly today?
Does it mean that it understands
me, that today I start
to lose all?

Like autumn leaves settling quietly
on the grass
on the boughs
along the field path
in the village,
does it mean that the wind
understands me, that today
I start to lose all?

Why is the wind
fretting so impatiently?
Does it mean that it understands
me, that I start to regain
all that I have lost?

THINGS LOST IN AUTUMN

Things lost in autumn:
The leaves dangling
On the tree-top in the street,
The sapling of a branch,
Green foliage.

Things lost in autumn:
The gentle breeze nestling
fleece-soft in the bosom,
Insects chirping under the scattered leaves,
The bell-sound vibrating
The walls at morn and even,
The lingering notes
From the old rusty bell.

Things lost in autumn:
Habit of handclasping in prayer
Which has formed since when God knows,
A mind willing to yield all
When demanded by God.

More precious things
Lost in autumn:
Multitudes of events and profound truths,
Humanity as a whole,
The heaven and the earth,
The whole universe,
And others as great.

Nevertheless
On second thought
What we have lost in autumn
Are mere trifles:

A part of man,
A section of a year,
A particle of a season rounded
With sentimentalism,
And shattered pieces so trivial,
Pieces of waste paper,
Crumbled bits of fallen leaves,
A cloud of dust rising,
Dust and dust
Nothing but dust.

THE FRUIT TREE

Can anything surprise me more
than the fruit maturing on a tree?

Taking root in poor red soil
its branches beaten by weather
the fruit tree chooses autumn
when things start to fall
for the glory of colors and a load of grace.

Can anything surprise me more
than the fruit maturing on a tree?

I drift the whole year away
harvesting no single poem.

But in autumn I recover my vision
at the miracle of the fruit tree.

TWO THEMES IN FANTASY

1. A Terrestrial Globe

I spin
A terrestrial globe
As I spin
A huge flower.

Multitudes of suns and moons
Scatter like so many sparks of fire
As petals drift
Upon my forehead.

I spin a flower
As I spin a chunk of earth.

Multitudes of seasons
Wheel in a whirl
As a colorful top
Spins upon the blue paper.

2. Man

If I could open you
As I open the door.

If I could enter you and lie down in you
As I open the door into the room and lie there.

If I could fasten you
As I fasten a button.

If I could lock you up
As I lock the door and lose its key.

Park, Pong'u (1934-1990)

Born in Kwangju, South Chŏlla Province, Park graduated from Chŏnnam University where he majored in Political Science. He was recognized as a poet with his prize-winning piece "The Truce Line" published in a newspaper in 1956. He received a couple of poetry prizes. His work includes *The Truce Line* (1957), *A Flower-tree That Blooms in Winter* (1959) and *A Grass-leaf in the Wasteland* (1976).

THE TRUCE LINE

Mountains face each other. Distrusting eyes glare
each other. Knowing that this volcano will explode any
day from the dark like a crash of thunder, should we
remain here helpless as flowers?

The chill landscapes stare each other. Shall we hear no
more in this lovely land the brave spirit sung of our
ancestors and the heroic legends of the ancient kingdoms?
The stars are happy to share the same skies; we are alone
pulled asunder, unable to slough off the gnawing agonies.

Blood no more bathes the land, but we are here in this
square from which no single tree is safe to grow. Our
old wounds still hurting us, is it a rest or an empty talk
that we are having?

O hateful wind like a viper's tongue, will you blow
bringing down the rigors of another winter? How long
can these innocent flowers live out their lives?
Is this the only beautiful choice left to us?

Mountains face each other. Distrusting eyes glare
each other. Knowing that this volcano will explode any
day from the dark like a crash of thunder, should we
remain here helpless as flowers?

WHAT DOES IT MATTER IF AZALEAS BLOW?

After the blood-gust of April*
took it by storm
the city looks unruffled
as if nothing ever happened.

What does it matter if azaleas blow?
Our hearts torn asunder
are stripped of will to life.

Toward sunset
the whole city,
incapable of suicide,
haunts every public house.

Delay taking your medicines
but listen to these sad stories;
look at these faces sunk and yellow.

Thanks to the youthful blood of April
every one I meet wears heroic medals
polluting the spirit of revolution.

The only place left to all
is a padded cell
in the hospital.

Listen, all suicide groups,
hoist your torn flag;
was it to this sad end that I shouted?

* Indicates the students' uprising which toppled a dictatorial government.

THE LAND FOREVER OUR OWN

I waited for love,
nothing but love.
The day the north wind was
stirring at dawn,
in a glitter of the sun,
I brought you to mind,
O homeless one.
Love blazes up like fireworks.
I board a north-bound train
or walk along the rusty railroad.
This land, our eternal home,
is silent, stained with bloodmarks.

Kwŏn, Ilsong (1933-)

Born in Sunchang, North Chŏlla, Kwŏn studied engineering at Chonnam University. He came to establish himself as a poet with his prize-winning piece "Sleepless Badge" coming out in a newspaper in 1957. He has three books of poems to his credit. They include *This Land Makes Me Drink* (1966), *Slash-and-Burn People in the City* (1969) and *The Woman of the Sea* (1982).

MEMORY OF THE SEINE

Autumn was a wharf,
gone in a flutter,

making a woman, back turned,
and the nude trees cry
preparing its own cry
ready for more things.

Even the mountains flow by
if seen from the sea.
Where the mountains and people float by
memories stop short:
loss that makes one feel good,
inevitable bitterness of innocent suffering.

La seine!
La seine!

The collapse of autumn is in fact
a relation between birth and death.

THE APOCALYPSE

At 7 p.m. at Kwanghwamun
when a bottle of gin is finished with roast beef
night gyrates to cast a spell
over us, her and me.

At the base of a cliff
where one day's summarized career
lies limp, water-wet,
my eager hand edges its way
along the Monte Carlo beach
till it shuttles in and out of her womb.

I hear her heart on fire.
Her burning frame, sharp in her appetite,
wriggles like a serpent,
gripping my limbs as in a vise,
when a start signal
launches our capacity loaded ship.

What fun, My Eve!
I kiss repeatedly
to commemorate my occupation
of your citadel.
Who can blame what we are up to?

An apple glows red, bestial
by my bedside;
sunk into the mire of suggestive night
I float in midair,
my dangling neck suspended in the void.

FOR COAL'S SAKE

Coal is burning.
Making a mockery of ever-smiling years
A center is burning.

Glaring light
Nautical lane of frayed edge
General fatigue that illuminates
the world to its end

Anger held rather in quiet
Oh, Alaska sunk into the swamps!
Oh, plains of coarse food!
All things of this world burn.
All that burns is reduced to ashes.

The annoying night grows mellow.
The present is always
the sunlight of an alien country,
ailing with general fatigue and nausea.

There is a wind of labor
that erects the first dawn of a winter day
on a plow-edge.

A shovelful of coal
dug out from Samch'ŏk and Toge
and from a coal mine in the Ruhr
intensely moves us.

It lets hair grow in the heart
in dribs and drabs
the amount of daily lethal dose.

Coal is burning
Sweat streaming on a thousand feet underground.
The strength of arms bracing up as if possessed.

The concentrated eyebeams
open in resurrection.

The worn-out soul
melts the frozen mountains and valleys
The briquet holes tied to the hearth
in the kitchen cluttered up with bread and guillotines.
Light glows through the aisles between the holes.

Listening to the tale of the brawny men;
the war of tears shed by those men;
Listening to the tale of their women
and the fetuses in the wombs of those women
I give thought to the home of the coal
that moves us intensely green

Go to Samch'ŏk.
Go to Toge.
Go to the coal mines in Ruhr and Duisburg,

Alas!
The edge of warm death
The statement of freedom thrown away
Songs and demonstrations
shrunk like the eyebrows
of a bastard
born of this age.

Even in the depth of the ground
dawns the morning of plows,
dawns the morning of clanking metal,
rousing the sound of shovels in the slumbering labor.

Love is not love which doesn't burn.
Faith is not faith which doesn't burn.
Life is not life which doesn't burn.

Coal is burning.

Yu, Kyŏnghwan (1936-   )

Born in Chang'yŏn, Hwanghae Province in North Korea, Yu graduated from
Yonsei University. He spent one year at East-west Center in Hawaii. His recogni-
tion as a poet came in 1958 when his first poems were published in *Hyondae
Munhak* (Modern Literature). Currently, he works for the Choson Daily as an
editorial writer. His work includes *Emotional Map* (1969), *Sunset in the Moun-
tains* (1972), *The Black Sun* (1974), *In the Classical Snowfield* (1975), *This Small
Bird of Mine* (1977) and *Birds and October* (1979).

RAINY WEATHER

Stone wall fallen under rainy weather.
Each morning I pile up a few stones to mend it.
Often I wonder which should go where it belongs.
I pick up the stones to be duly placed back
and stretch my back with joy at discovering right
ones for the right places but fine it hard to
place them, duly back by the sound of the stones
in my hand and I stroke the duly placed stones
which smile showing their black teeth in a row.
Awakening comes with ordeal each morning as I
pile up forty years of stones and hesitate as I
stretch my back because nothing has been achieved.
And yet each morning when I meet up with ordeal
I put it off till tomorrow and wash my dirty hands.

HARVEST

In the golden stubble of paddy field
Rows of lions sit on their haunches
After a summer of racing the plains;
Now meek and broken-in
Maturing through the whole summer
They virtuously yield to their Master.

Though the far-off ridges
Start burning in bright flame
Their eyes closed,
Held armful against the farmer's body
They are loaded in the cart.
A pride of lions.

ON THE BEACH

In a silk rustle she sheds her scales
diffidently hugging the sound of the sea
that rolls in and out along the shoreline

The sleek curvature slaloms down her
shy armpits, silhouetting against the sunset
Across the swells of the abyss
storm waits beyond the horizon

Gold sands spangle on the nude surface

Fever-driven she sheds her scales,
the nude, motor-boat starts its engine
after sundown

Sŏng, Ch'unbok (1934-   )

Born in Sangju, South Kyŏngsang, Sŏng studied Korean literature at Sung-gyungwan University. His first poems came out in *Hyondae Munhak* (Modern Literature) in 1958. Currently he teaches at a number of colleges. His work includes *An Inland Trip* (1960), *The Pagoda Park* (1966), *A Lyric Song* (1970), *A Festival for Peach Blossoms* (1982) and *For the Outside World* (1985).

I LIVE HERE

I live here
for the love of this land
I stay here so that I can
call and answer the land
from her towering mountain peaks
down to the depths of her rivers.

High winds may rise
knocking off lovely flowers;
blocking the roads across the land
yet I prefer to live here
under the blue of heaven
where her bright smiles
clear the overcast skies.

Locked in by a narrow
strip of land
from one end to the other
I live here
for the love of this land
for a taste of fresh spring water.

TEA AT DAWN

Between dark and light
I make tea,
dawn's gate fastened.

For a cupful of water
night gives us rain;
fog clears from the way.

Out of mire of dreams
life brightens at dawn;
I rise only to sit again.

The shadow that darkens
my empty tea cup
startles me into hiding behind the door.

THE SONG OF STORM

It was a wind, a peal of thunder,
a storm in the autumn night
sweeping across the sandy flats in my heart.

It was a creamy white bird in the nest,
up in an old tree in the woods,
pluming itself, refusing to give in to grief.

It was the sound of rain in the darkness,
a violent flow of air tossing
our ship like mad.

We depart from the port that slumbers in peace,
and I fear our ship may sink
before a touch of rippling waves.

Now there's no wind, darkness unveiled.
Nor is my way found on the seas
that ebb in and out.

Shin, Tong'yŏp (1930-1969)

Born in Pyuŏ, South Ch'ungchŏng Province, Shin studied history at Konkuk University and majored in Korean literature as a graduate student. He established himself as a poet with his prize-winning piece "The Earth of a Plowman who Talks" in 1959 in a newspaper. His work includes *Women of Asia* (1963), an epic *The River Kum* (1967) and *Selected Poems*, posthumously published.

AZALEAS FLOODING THE LANDSCAPE

A few flowering azaleas dotting the roadside,
a common butterfly poised on a rock's edge,
you've gone to the last sleep, a rifle
thrown down on the grass.

On that spot where the rock lies
generals had buried their men, it's been said,
in the sun bright days of old,
in the days of the late Koguryo dynasty.*

Those languished while waiting died in the mountains,
their bones in a heap taking the mountainside
by force like flowers in blossom.

You would roll a cigarette, I remember, smiling a cheerless
    smile;
You said your blind folks left behind by the south sea
would go hungry.

I have just seen someone's
amputated ankle stuck in a boot
on the sandy patches in the orchard.

All day long bullets were raining
down the flowering mountainside.

Those languished while waiting died in the mountains.
Onto the flowering mountainside
bullets were raining down all day.

A few flowering azaleas dotting the roadside,
An Adonis lay cold and dead in the rock shade.

A plane flew over us to machine-gun
the flowering village and was gone.

Those languished while waiting died in the mountains,
their longing flaring up heavenward,
their bones taking the mountainside by force.

On that spot where the rock lies
generals had buried their men, it's been said,
in the days of the late Koguryo dynasty,
in the days of warm wind blowing.

You lay bleeding in quiet,
your cigarette case thrown down on the grass.

* The late Koguryo (901-918) was founded by Kungye, assumedly a son of King Honan, the 47th king of the Silla dynasty. Lasting only eighteen years, it was subjugated by Wang-gon, the founder of the Koryo dynasty.

ON THE HILLS AND MOUNTAINS

His dear familiar face is no more to be seen;
his favorite flowers will bloom,
so bright on the hills and mountains.

The sweet song he used to sing is no more heard;
his clear voice will remain alive in the fields and woods.

O lonely wanderer traversing the fields,
Fill with wind should the snow-road be empty,
Fill with tenderness should the wind be empty.

His dear familiar looks are no more to be seen;
his spirit that departed in tears
will flower in the fields and woods.

HUSK, BE GONE

Husk, be gone;
April,* let your husk
go and your grain remain.

Husk, be gone;
Let only the shouting
of the Tonghak revolution**
remain, its husk gone.

And again, husk, be gone
from this land
in which a native lad meets his lass,
heart to heart,
free and easy;
they will welcome each other
for the marriage of minds
in the peace hall
of neutrality.

Husk, be gone
from Mount Halla in the south
to Mount Paektu in the north;
Let all glinting metals go
and only sweet earth remain.

* Allusive to the students' uprising which toppled a dictatorial regime in April, 1959.
** Referring to the Peasant Uprising against the corrupted government in 1894.

Hong, Yun'gi (1933-)

Born in Seoul, Hong went to Hankuk University of Foreign Studies where he studied English. He established himself as a poet with his first poems published in *Hyondae Munhak* (Modern Literature) in 1959. In the same year he was winner of the poetry contest sponsored by a newspaper. At present he works for the Korea Broadcasting Station. Since his first poems came out, Hong has continually been at work on his poems. He is now planning to collect all his poems in book form.

THUNDER

At night after the festival
of royal azaleas on Mount Chiri
all had dropped to sleep
overwhelmed by fatigue
before sudden sheetings of rain
and maddening claps of thunder
swayed me awake: I had to sit up, frightened.

The mountain deity
with all the peaks under his thumb
was venting his wrath, it seemed,
flagellating the earth with a vengeance.

Fact was he stormed
urging us to repent of our sins
that blacken our souls.

CRIMSON MAPLES

A gang of spirited children
with ruddy faces keep shouting
as they clamber up the cliffside

Forceful in their vocal bands
they shout
igniting the whole mountains

They are devoured by fire
burning red-hot
like a volcanic eruption

Catching on fire
wrapped in burning mountains
I shout and shout in company

A FLY BALL

A hand stuck pat
in the blue of the sky;

it is a white ball flashing
launched by burning passion,
an explosive shouting.

What a delight to the spectators
as against their hitless daily lives!
I feel like rolling about in the green ground.

Kim, Yŏngt'ae (1936-)

Born in Seoul, Kim went to Hongik University where he majored in fine arts. His recognition came with "Snow Piece" published in a magazine in 1959. His poems tend to explore the psychological region of human situations. He has three books of poems to his credit: *The Village of the Jews* (1965), *Mean Ratio* (1968) in collaboration with others and *Cigarettes for the Guests* (1978).

HOTEL NORTH

A couple of angels get in,
the door closed behind them.
Made of paper, neither of them
can pull at the other
nor knock the other down.
The building itself is of paper,
its staircase hand-folded with paper;
a single step
will send it crashing flat.
The water in the paper vase
is blue indeed.
As it's fresh from the spring;
there's no use worrying
if the flowers in the vase will fade.
The only thing that stirs with life
is the water that ripples
or the flower that drops its
beautiful petals, one by one.

A SNOWFLAKE

What's your part
in 'The Nutcracker Suite'?
Just moving things
behind the main roles
My role merely being one
of the myriad snowflakes
continually falling from the heavens
only to disappear
Moments designed to perish

Like children
I reach out my face
for the heaven
arms carefree folded back
They fall continually toward me
thickly drifting
Remain sky-floated after disappearance
I will hold on to its bluishness

LANDSCAPE

A lake comes in sight
A swan floats on it
Fairly good
Boughs of trees are mirrored in the water
I often tremble
despite my firm hold on the heart
I cannot help it
Swan floats in a corner
The currents slumber
All is fairly good
And yet I am alone
all in a tremble
I immediately realize a sign
that something has sunk or
gone crumbling in my heart

BUTTERFLY

Past grassland
butterfly
is crossing the stepping stones
Though it looks back again and again
sky is serene like a stage backdrop
While crossing the stepping stones
It is caught in a second of hesitation
It flutters
in the confines of my palm
Butterfly
is in a tremble
trembling spreads and stops
Looks like a mysterious color;
a piece of cloth unendingly transparent

Hwang, Tonggyu (1938-   )

Born in Seoul, Hwang studied English literature at Seoul National University where he presently teaches. He went to Edinburg University for a year's research. His poems in general are an attempt to seek his identity in the vortex of realities. His work includes *A Certain Clear Day* (1961), *Rain Falling in the South* (1975), *When I See a Wheel I Want to Roll It* (1978), *Wind Burial* (1984) and *Who Is Afraid of Alligators?* (1986).

A LITTLE LOVE SONG

A letter came with yesterday tied to it.
The path I would follow you along
has suddenly gone out of sight;
gone too are those things
other than the road.
The pebbles we used to play with
anywhere as children are
scattered, stuck in the earth,
half hidden from view.
"I love you, I love you."
In the chill glow of evening sky
I see gold slowly beaten into a yellow dome;
now swirl in thin flakes as if
reluctant to land on the ground.
A flake or two roam endlessly
seized by insomnia.

ELEGY

—11th song—

I sing a winter port;
the melancholy of midwinter;
—snow drifts about
in the dark wharf—
the massed night
of a shipless port;
the tiny stars that adorn
awhile the mute isles.
When a sliced moon sank;
you're gone away
I could hear the sound
of billows backwashing,
pulled by the moon;
the shaking of a big wet circle

Think quietly
of your heart in which dwells
a poor little boy whose face
resembles the girlhood face
of St. Anne immortalized
by da Vinci;
behind him stand
a hamlet planted by an old thatched house
and a few saplings
driving him to the port
in a gesture of denial.
Snow drifts about in the port.
Think quietly of
a day in the port;
the nets ripped apart;
tackle, seaweeds, safe arrival of some fish,
a few capsized wooden boats
and a tavern nailed with fishbones.

Think quietly of
a few nights;
a sleep like a temporary railroad;
a sleep that comes in belly not in brain.
After the departure of the last ship
light is out.

I know
we are not something incapable of comparison.
I know
we are something simple, something yearned for,
like roots of a wild flower
whose name I do not know
pitifully accompanying it
as I pull it out.
I know
the length of the roots
that accompany all departures;
a sleep of those who possess a map
and the dim lamplight that guards their faces,
Unendingly on a spring day
I just stand in a wistful desire,
lamp in hand.

A LESSER LOVE SONG

A few scraps of the wind
that has not ceased to blow
The wet snow that settles down
at supper-time or a waterdrop
that keeps running in a runnel
dissolves in midair before a fall
A waterdrop brushes by you
drawn from one wind to another
as you suddenly spread your arms

SEA GULLS

something that sounds like a song
where wings flap in a surge

a beautiful distance
that flies out from water's depth to water's depth

I also wished to cry a smile
not sad nor happy,
a cry like a passing cloud

a beautiful distance
that flies out from water's depth to water's depth

1960s and 1970s

Kim, Huran (1934-   )

Born in Seoul, Kim attended Teachers College, Seoul National University. Her recognition as a poet came in 1960 when her poems were published in *Hyondae Munhak* (Modern Literature). She worked for daily newspapers as a reporter and then as an editorial writer. At present she heads Women Development Institute. Her work includes *Ornamental Knife and Rose* (1968), *Musical Scale* (1971), *Certain Waves* (1976) and *Collected Poems* (1985).

WINTER TREE

The tree keeps silence,
eyes clammed shut,
lost in deep thoughts.

As if to flash back light
I turn into a tree,
tossing silence in response.

The wind stirs.
The cold moon passes a wakeful night
in mossed silence.

When no one anticipates the oncoming spring
the tree tells me what it is like
to wait with patience.
The spring is nesting in my heart.

MOUNTAIN

A band of self-respect
girding the uprising summit
It stares at the seas
shimmering for millions of years

Smoothing down its robe-end
folded in ruffles
it zen-meditates for a whole day
only eyebrows bristling

Even a violent gesture
and a variety of shadows
remain behind the sound of silence
Winds would open the heaven's gate
shuttling between the past and the future

But at this very moment
when cold rain-drops
soak the roots
hand strokes the flapping wings
of a fledgling bird
warm hand moves tenderly

TO BE IN TIME FOR MASS

I wait for the night.
Time breaks my back.
At the edge of something about to change
a hairy beast passes by rubbing its behind
on the world telescoped to a snapshot.
Flocks of ducks leave their waddly effotprints.
Tender grass-flowers heave a heavy sigh,
The black habit wreathes the priest's neck.
The faceless night closes in, velvet-soft,
its breaths stroking the hair beneath my ears.
I smile
and step hurriedly into the picture
to be in time for a mass.

FISH COOKING

The sea has invaded the kitchen.
The waves surge on a chopping board.

To remove its coat of mail
that challenges the sun;
to chop it into several cuts
takes a certain measure of courage.

The world has already gone eye-shut.
Against the staircase
that slopes seaward
the waves foam sprawling,
knife blades held between their teeth.

Shin, Kyŏngnim (1936-   )

Born in Chung'wŏn, North Ch'ungch'ŏng Province, Shin studied English at Dong-guk University. Shin's poems in general concern misery, anger, regrets, and bitter-ness of the farming population. His work includes *Farmers' Dance* (1973) and *The Ridge* (1979).

A VISIT TO A RURAL TOWN

A market day it was, more deserted
than any other day;
droughts had dried up paddy fields enough to raise dust;
roofs and stone walls languished as farmers.

Our bus stopped at a trade post
that overlooks my wife's grave in the distance.
I took my son into a roadside stall
where we drank tepid drinks
manufactured by foreign capital.

Meeting my friends I hadn't seen for long
I wondered why their eyes were shot with blood.
Silent,
They just shook my hand,
a forced smile painted on their faces.

The chicken-house lane was littered
with stones, sticks, and hoes.
I remember that place facing the barber's
where peasants and miners would shout
curses in a fight;
a walk lined with rice dealers;
the volunteer fire fighters
who would scramble down the lane.

A market day it was, deserted than any other day.
Horny hands held my hand tight
as if reluctant to let me go
the day I came to visit my wife's grave.

THAT DAY

A young woman weeps
following a hearse alone.
No streamer or hand-bell.
The smoke-spreading evening road
is darkened by specter shadows.
Onto the street, unwindowed, undoored,
the wind drifts leaves off the roadside trees.
People watch hiding behind the trees
and utility poles.
No one knows the name of the dead.
It's a dark, moonless night.

REED

Reed had been weeping
Silently and inwardly
Since when no one knows
Until one fine night
He suddenly realized
That his whole frame was swaying

It wasn't wind nor moonbeams
But his own weeping
That caused his shaking,
He knew nothing about it.

To live is to weep
Silently and inwardly,
He did not know before.

THE DIARY OF A MOUNTAIN TOWN

Should we live as listlessly as we do now?
On a night when it snows
I cannot get to sleep.
Mr. Pak in a ward, Brother Song
in his sickbed and I idling
beside my thin wife
who has cut her arm;
parted from one another
should we just listen to
the snow crunching on the roof?
I give a thought to the local poet
who was kidnapped to the north and
his wife now married to another man.
Should we live as listlessly as we do now?
In this mountain town?
With pay virtually snatched from
children's pocket money
I buy briquets, I drink,
I play a game of cards in the night-duty room
and think of the unfortunate poet;
of his daughter who limps in the legs.
Should we just listen to a dog
barking in a far-off village?
Should we just listen to the train
rattling on the rails?
On a snowing night when our friends
go mad, die from madness,
should we live as listlessly as we do now
in this mountain village?

THE RIVER

Rain is sobbing in streaks.
It gets stuck sobbing in the mud.
Children flee from the rain.

Has the river forgotten the cry?
The gun reports and the shoutings?
The little fists and the bare feet?

Wind is sobbing.
It circles sobbing over the river.
Children wander behind the wind.
They wander sobbing in the pouring rain.

THAT SUMMER

One man's cry
called in a crying to the whole village.
One man's song
Drove a singing to the whole village;
the clouds
winds and rain;
called in flowers and a dancing;
curses, profanities and bitterness.

One man's song
Drove a singing to the whole village
and one man's death
called in a death to the whole nation.

Shin, Tongchun (1931-   )

Born in Sinŭiju, North Korea, she went to Ehwa Women's University where she
majored in English Literature. Her recognition as a poet came in 1966 when her
first poems were published in *Hyondae Munhak* (Modern Literature). Her work
includes *A Certain Day* (1970), *Tenacity and Thereafter* (1976), *From Distance to
Hypothesis* (1980) and *Flower Petals Raining Down Against the Sky* (1985). Cur-
rently she teaches English Literature at Hanyang University.

LIFE

Just one single touch
May let it go to pieces;
Or be lost for good
As in a blazing flame;
I keep it up day by day.

Despite my frailty
(overlooked by none)
I have had a thousand nights
Sleepless, eyes open or shut;
I will pray for you with good grace.

The candle burning with a hiss
Into the last wisp of its spirit
Shines around where life breathes;
Where its breaths pulsate
In a gushing thirst.

Gather these jewels suddenly fallen apart;
String those rainbow hues
On your silken thread.
Burnt out or battered to bits,
It stands its stubborn ground
With its colors firm and enduring.
That is what life is like.

IN AUTUMN

We love deeper in autumn
because the sky gets bluer.

Occasionally we stop by the roadside
to watch the tree-tops wavering ahead;

we like to shake our heads hoping
to shake down our unripe thoughts;

we like to come to our old campus
desiring to be like the salvias blazing there.

I'LL BE WITH YOU

A path in the woods is so lovely
bathed in the showering sunlight.

Shedding my chronic scruples
I take the road to meet you,
like a submissive bride,
into the cascades of light
even the shuttered eyes can see by.

Don't look around
or you will turn to stone,
a column of salt
or you'll become a prey to a tiger.

I am coming to you
with the burning sun on my head.

VOICE

When no one forgives me;
the north wind no more nips me;
when I lost count of the silver coins
for which Judas betrayed his Lord,
I strike the road
in search of you
as a miner goes prospecting for ore.

Face, name and age lost to memory,
voice alone rings suddenly in my ears.
The sound of wind fills the empty plains
in which I stand cooling my heels
in the invading darkness.
I sense your presence
somewhere beyond where a dog barks;
somewhere under the brightest star.

Kim, Yangshik (1931-   )

Born in Seoul, Kim graduated from Ehwa Women's University where she studied English Literature. At graduate school in Dong-guk University she majored in Indian Literature and philosophy. Currently she directs the Korean-Indian Literature Association. Her work includes *The Song of Chong'up* (1969), *Collected Poems* (1974) and *A Tomcat* (1980).

BECAUSE THERE

In the crack of a thickly mossed rock
at the base of a hill
a spear of grass wavers
with a tiny white flower balanced on its head.
I do not know what it is called,
shy and slim in the neck.

The nondescriptive vegetation on a darkened rock
must be aged billions of years, it seems.
A sudden cry of a cuckoo
matches the sound of wind in God-like harmony
because
they know how to follow nature's way.

ELEGY

Because of you I have lived
because of your call I have lived
O my love
O my love

My voiceless shouting
that stabs the sky
no more reaches you now
but condenses into snow
piling on the peaks far out
drifting back into the ancient times

GRASS FLOWER

Remembering those far-off days I have
    passed lonely
I sit now in a rocker, my eyes closed

Each of us shall be a flower of grass
Or a grass blade

Again I shall die
Only to be another grass flower
Or grass blade lying breathless in sorrow

I shall lie down on the grass blade
And pluck a grass flower

In thought of those innocent days
I sit in a rocker, my eyes closed

Come tenderness so gentle
And I will let you go with a kiss

The grass flower ripples
Sorrow onto my heart
I tiptoe skyward
To hug the scented wind whirling

I shall perish only to be a grass flower
On the grass blade I lie down
And pluck a grass flower

ON AN AUTUMN MORNING

My eyes chance to rest on my husband's hair.
The morning sun at the moment reveals an
amazing abundance of white.

How fleeting were these many years!

In small space the width of a hand-span
Each of us has been dreaming a different dream,
Seemingly familiar yet forever unknown to the other.
Taking the other for granted, most intimate friend

By the window on a quiet autumn morning
When another is not far behind
My eyes suddenly rest on his hair
which glistens in the morning sun;
I see there the coming years come as fast
as they have passed.

A LINE OF VERSE

Soundless,
Time allotted to us flows
and becomes a weight a thousand stones heavy
only to press my bruised heart

Blood stands in stasis
Thought stands still

Wakeful nights
darkening days
flow unendingly until
the tip of a thin orchid blade,
my life, its edge sharpened green,
a cold thread of verse,
flashes
and . . .

Kim, Yŏjŏng (1933-   )

Born in Chinju, South Kyŏngsang Province, Kim graduated from Korean Litera-
ture department at Sunggyungwan University. She also studied at Kyonghee Uni-
versity at graduate school level. Her recognition came with her first poems being
published in *Hyondae Munhak* (Modern Literature) in 1968.

Her work includes *Harmony* (1969), *Sunlight Pouring down on the Sea* (1973)
and *The Sea of Lemon* (1976).

STONE

Off the promontory at Pusan
riding on a green-jade wave
only to turn into the wave
my second and third sons
get driven onto the shore,
glittering, turned into green jade

Running into deer's antlers
that bristle in a stony patch
I tore down my chastity kept for a decade

Over the ravishing love-making of their mother
the second and the third sons
were standing as bridemaids
They fetched a cut of the sea
and covered us from sight, from sight.

The waves too
were grinning at our togetherness
their hands clapping

LABYRINTH

My niece past marriageable age
and I much older than she
strolled arm in arm
on the Chongno street
in early summer morning
more than crystal clear
and we pushed open a door
of an exclusive jeweller's
to get side by side
into the turquoise of heaven

Browsing through the garden
overgrown with ruby
next to the mossed woods of emerald
my niece past marriageable age
lost herself into a one-karat diamond
while I was circling inside a pair
of pure gold rings
in search of her lost and gone
when I caught sight of moon and stars and dew
and found her turned to moon, to star
or dew until she came out blinded
in many years of being locked inside
a piece of jewel
at the brilliant rays of sun
on the summit of Mont Blanc
only to fall into Lake Leman

where she was coral-swaying
before she was hauled out
from Helios' gold net
and fell asleep lying on the sands
as she was spinning a dream of opal
with waves rolling in and out
over the white soles of her feet.

By the time Alexandrian port wine
became mature in the hollow navel
of my neice drenched in the waves
I came, bedevilled by flame and flood,
to shake her into awakening
from the world beyond
until she came to
her eyes opening brightly
like a gardenia in the moonlight.

THE SEA OF LEMON

From flower that captures more
from love that captures me
from God who controls me
from lemon smell that captivates me
I wish to be released
I wish to bleed in released agony

To bleeding enemy
to bleeding angel
to bleeding lemon meat
I wish to give a kiss
I wish to tremble to loneliness that kisses

Wounded lemon
in the bleeding sea
I wish to salvage the thick summer foliage
in the wake of a martyred death

IN THE SUMMER

In the summer
love too goes to the mountains
In the summer
love too goes to the sea
In the streets
no single flower of love flames red

In the summer
death too goes to the mountains
In the summer
death too goes to the sea
In the streets
no single leaf of death falls

Friend, in the summer
your love and mine
go to the mountains
overgrown with your death and mine
Your death and mine
go to the sea
where your love and mine have drowned

In the skies all over
no single flag that bleeds
No single despair that dazzles
In the summer
O friend!

Hŏ, Seuk (1934-   )

Born in Imsil, Chŏnbuk Province, Hŏ studied Chinese literature at Han Kuk University of Foreign Studies, and at Taiwan National Normal University where he obtained a Ph.D. Currently he teaches at Hankuk University of Foreign Studies. Hŏ started writing poetry in Chinese since the 1960s and his poems in Korean came out after 1969. His books of poems include *The Blue Awning* (1979), *The River Flowing under the Ground* (1980), and *Ode to Snowflakes* (1986) in Chinese.

SOMETHING GREATER THAN HEAVEN

Who calls me
I go out into barren emptiness
only to find a wind in the hollow corner
burrowing into the earholes of dandelions?

Who calls me
that I stand on the grass
where the crescent moon is moored awhile
I hear the dews dropping down
captured in the starry field all night long?

Who calls me
that when I feel the rail of dusking twilight
I hear the skeletons of leaven fallen last year
undulate their waists for a crawl?

Who calls me
that I cannot hear a sound
greater than the bell-sound when I come close to the hill
where the bell sounds?

Who calls me that
as I go farther into emptiness
I find something greater emptied
something greater than heaven emptied

THE BELL

Into the sky where a kite has fled
Tolls the bell in waves, its sound bonging
in search of the lost kite

Like a burst of wailing that rumbles back
alone in echo, like a plunge into depth
for the loss of jewels dearest to the heart.

Billowing waves tossed in a curl draw a circle
as they crush to potsherds an iron bridge.
In the quiet of a hermitage nestled in an
autumn mountain that shouts in a crimsoning voice
dozes a broomstick, worn to a stump.

In an impatient wait for the last word
the snowdrifts burst into a weep that
galvanizes a procession of nirvana-vehicles.

Thick mist spreads.
In the thickness of mist the bell gropes
in a quiver for a speech sound.

IN THE RAIN AND WIND

When winds blow
Let hungry people meet one another
When rain falls
Let the sightless birds gather together

Up in a glassed-in attic that opens into space
wearing wind
counting rain

Aren't these the steps to heaven
I have so long longed to ascend?

With an umbrella unfolded
hunger-ridden shoulders creaking
Let the sightless birds walk along

Kim, Jaihiun (1934-   )

Born in Kwangju, the provincial capital of South Chŏlla, Kim studied English at Hankuk University of Foreign Studies. He received training in creative writing at the University of Massachusetts where he earned two graduate degrees. He taught English and creative writing in an American college before returning home to Korea in 1971. Kim's poems in English started to be published in the 1960s in the United States. His poems in Korean were first published in 1975. Currently, Kim teaches at Ajou University. His books of poetry comprise nine volumes including *Detour* (1972) and *A Pigsty Happiness* (1973), both in English, *Revolt of Soil* (1975), *Drifting Life* (1979), *Dancing Weeds* (1982) and *A Certain Hug* (1986). In addition, Kim has so far translated more than 2000 Korean poems into English.

MOTHER-THOUGHT

Her face,
geography of sorrows,
buffeted by head winds,
through the harshness of years,
turned into a plaster image.

Gentleness in her eyes
reminding me of Bodhisattva
ripples into my memory,
generosity radiating.

Hers was a simple wish:
to see a famed temple.
What if they ask me about it, she said,
once across the eternal river?

Foolishness of her son
to mock her simple heart.
Caught in the whirligig of human affairs,
free-wheeling for years,
grasping void after void,
she turned into a plaster image.

Her face,
geography of sorrows.

TO A NIGERIAN FRIEND

Material voluptuousness vexed you.
You saw through the emptiness of luxury.
Progress wasn't equal to comfort.
Stranded by choice onto the soil to which
your ancestors had been sold as slaves
you commanded lifted eyes and pride
from the heart for what your African
heritage stood for. Far from pretensions
you offered me what you were and I was happy
to return your gift in kind.
We must have been of one blood
and flesh in a former life
or rather we are part of the master spirit
in man.

LEGACY

Asked by a friendly neighbor
my own son's age
what my native place is like

I should say straight from the shoulder
it's where azaleas blow,
scop-owls fluting in springtime.

Asked again
where on earth it can be,
my answer would be it's where you give for love;

you may not see it for I have etched
it in my memory.
My tight-fisted friend stands agape,
hard-bitten by distrust.

Now I ask myself
how to plant this flower-spirit
into his soul thickly coated with comfort-rust.

THE LAW OF FALL

The mist enfolding the mountainside
condenses into dewdrops;
the rocks loaded down by a heap of a thousand years
go loose in running sandgrains.

A young bonze, now a canonized high priest,
sees his own frame blazing on a pyre,
ending his earthly existence.

In the far-away ravine of life
all past years seem but yesterday.
The red-flaming apple
and the lark stabbing the blue heaven
are doomed to drop to the ground
with the oncoming nightfall;
the snowflakes in a frolic whirling
settle quietly toward twilight.

Like a meteorite stuck cold in earth
after shooting splendidly across the sky
all struggles and strifes
submit to the law of fall.

WONDER

Rusty cans heaped high on the bank
of a stream rolling through the city;
sails rigged up on the corner
of skid-row.

Nightless brightness of a dormitory;
undergraduates step in the algebra
of turtle-on-the-back lyrics,
like crickets singing.

Some distance from the noisy den
a leaf unhooks itself from old attachments
and falls, pinned-moth, upon the pool.
Silence hangs like a thought.

Kim, Chiha (1941-   )

Born in Mokpo, a port city in South Chŏlla Province, Kim studied Aesthetics at
Seoul National University. His first poems came out in *Shi-in* (Poet) in 1969.
During the 1970s and the early 1980s he was imprisoned due to his radical politi-
cal activism against the dictatorial regime. His "Five Thieves" is a poignant attack
on those involved in corruption. His work includes *Loess* (1970), *In Burning
Thirst* (1981), *Great Narrative: South* (1982) and *Longing for the Last Piece of Flesh*
(1991). He was awarded in 1975 the Lotus Prize by Asian and African Writers and
another prize by Poetry International in 1981.

BIRD

The azure of sky spreads over
the fluffy clouds and the glittering hills.
Bird on the wing,
why do you make me sad,
tearing my heart in chains?

Let me sink my teeth
in the innermost layer of my flesh;
blood flows from a wound
caused by my nightlong clawing
and it rots on hot summer's day.

Break loose the earth-bound frame,
just for once, night or day.
My sad eyes and blood-soaked body
have become too weakened to endure any longer.
O bird, hear these chains clang.

How long before I'll become thee?
O bird that flies freely across my soul's field
where thin light goes dimm
against the bright rays of day!

Now you flee from the blue edge of heaven
beyond the blue mountains.
Why do you make me sad,
tearing my heart in chains?
Fleeting clouds glitter endlessly.

AERIN I*

The bird cried only once
before it fled.
How my heart leaps!
O the morning sun that brightens fulgently
for a fleeting moment before it fades!
How could I know the glistening dews
choke my heart in joy?
Once
only for a single day
or for an hour
I did love you
with a true love
but how could I ever know
you've been sustaining me all the way
for these many years,
Aerin,
both my eyes and hands torn off.

Now both my legs chopped off,
reduced to a dump of garbage
from which shows red innocent proud flesh.

Aerin!
Aerin!
I call you, Aerin.

* Suggestive of ideal, love, pity, hope, etc.

AERIN 4

There was a time when I could
hardly bring myself to say
"I'm lonely."
Now I should speak
in a loud voice
into the hollow of heaven
"I'm lonely."

Gleams of light that
sweep across my breast;
between those rays thin shafts
gleam in and out and pass
through the days that are gone.
The more they pass,
the thinner they become.
And it hurts me.

Though I have a big mouth for speech
there's no one alive on earth
I can talk to now.
Though I clench my fist
there's nothing any longer
to be held in my hand.

There's no trace of longing
left in this place; the night rain is falling
and a note wafting from the blind flutist
makes me this lonely.

Chŏng, Hyŏnjong (1939-   )

Born in Seoul, Chŏng graduated from Yonsei University, where he studied phi-
losophy. He had been affiliated with journalism as a reporter before he took up
teaching at Seoul Junior College for Arts. His first poems were published in
Hyondae Munhak (Modern Literature) in 1965. His books are *The Dream of
Things* (1972), *Festivity of Suffering* (1974), *I Am Uncle Star* (1978) and *There Is an
Island between People* (1991).

RAPPORT

Night has lit the streetlamp
as if it were his own thoughts.

Fog has galvanized its
red glowing sentiments.

Fog's soggy tongue
and lamp's idle tongue
suck up each other's thinnest voice
the pathetic attraction of desire.

THE ABYSS OF SOUND
   — 4 Silence —

I watch a heap of quietness
lying fallen, soaked in blood.
Quietness was once the light,
quietness itself
or silence's dear comrade-in-arms.

I watch a group of silence.
Speech and silence
biting each other's tail
watch for a chance,
watch desperately as if they were
deadly enemies to each other.

NOTE 25

When a person cannot dispense with something
we say he is addicted to it. A dope fiend, for
instance, cannot go a single day without drug.
None of us, however, who cannot go foodless
are said to be food-addicts. I for one feel myself
addicted to food, for I can hardly stand a single day
on an empty stomach and so I must be a food-addict.
Narcotism is an offense against the law while food-
addiction or foodaholism is considered a lawful act
duly sanctioned by society. That is to say, a victory
of one form of addiction over another. Man's life,
in fact, is addicted to struggle, a victory-addiction.
In a hustle I wake up early today to go gloriously
to work so that I might hunt for daily bread, for
I am a foodaholic. Drugged with feeding myself,
I am an unmistakable addict.

MISERABLE

When I've finished a poem
I should bury it in the ground
or in the heaven.
Why should I be in a hurry to publish it?
O miserable me!
No matter how I try to hide myself
my shabbiness shows through my hide.

GOING BY FAR

Shall I go to the sea
and become a blowing sea-wind
or to a very cold climate
and turn to falling snow
or head to a warm territory
and be shining sunbeams
or go far west where the sunset
flushes, melting in the evening-glow?
This way life betrays itself in greatest beauty.

Yi, Kŭnbae (1940-)

Born in Tangjin, South Ch'ungch'ŏng Province, Yi graduated from the creative writing department at Sorabol Arts College. He writes both modern free verse and the sijo, traditional verses. His sijo won the prizes in spring poetry contests sponsored by major daily newspapers. He received a series of awards including The New Poets Prize from the Ministry of Culture and Information (1964). His work includes *Flower-tree Playing a Love-song* (1960), *O Song* (1981) and sijo poems *What the Stone Turtle Says in the East Sea* (1982).

A CERTAIN YEAR

"Alas! You have flown away like a mountain bird."
                                                        —Chiyong

There's something does not return once gone
Can a piece of rotten fruit flesh turn
to earth, to water or to wind?
The nature wails in a call
for something that never returns
Let me call back the evening tide of the village
where things mortal keep on living
The remaining life span of a wild flower
which has lived without a name
flares up in a blazing sound
somewhere on this cold winter day

A shaft of light filters through a papered window
Spoons clinking, laughing ruffling
Mother grows to be grandmother
Graves alone remain
Snow falls

THE VISION OF WINTER

With vision unable to reach the field edge
I watch the outdoors
where the mountain comes into being and perishes
and something which cannot come back to life
comes walking toward me,
a mass of sunlight,
a greenstuff thick with leaves,
you approach the door beating the snow off,
the incarnation of that mountain.
When I meet you, my throat cleared,
nothing is visible in the field;
I watch the field

THE SOUND OF WATER

The sound of water on which I pillowed my head
for a night sleep leaves Mt. Chiri for a fair in Kure town.
The sound of water heated by love like a fire of column
calls me "it snows" from behind;
the famed local tea odor tingling my tongue-tip,
the sound followed me standing seatless
aboard the express for Seoul
and shared my bed last night as my own blood and flesh
and goes to work this morning

DOOR

That I would lock the door
that I would think the crossbar
is loose as I lock the door
That I would have my eyes dazzled
before the surge of a flashlight,
half the door gone unhinged,
someone knocking in the middle of night
That I would sleep curled up
trembling like a flap of papered window
after the strangers were back
black footmarks left
on the open pages of my notebook
That I would wake on and off while asleep
That I would not trust my door

RISE AND FALL*

When asleep I always hear
the sea shout.
My dream rises and falls
on the waves.
When it dawns, I am a lonely
island far away from the shore.

This sad wreck of time
keeps lapping the shore.
My soul blows all night long
like a wind in the far distance.
When awake, all remains emptied,
rising and falling.

* A sijo poem.

Kang, Ushik (1941-)

Born in Chumunjin, Kangwŏn Province, Kang studied Korean Literature at Sunggyngwan University. His first poems came out in *Hyondae Munhak* (Modern Literature) in 1966. His work includes *Four-line Poems* (1973), *The Snowstorm in the Koryo Dynasty* (1973) and *Since I Began Plucking Flowers* (1979).

WORMWOOD

A frog is taking a sunbath
lying at full length on the wormwood;
I see a love-mad girl, turned to wormwood,
mirthfully revealing her white belly.

QUATRAIN ONE

Dear couples, our room is like an apple's interior
amid clear sunbeams that seep onto a baby's fingernail-tips.
Who would know us inhabiting its interior
spun secretly, pure from the external world?

QUATRAIN FIVE

Dead leaves hang on the twig-ends,
colored tissue paper crumpled away by a girl during her
menstruation.
O love, what can we do beside a girl
whose thought is deep as the grave?

QUATRAIN NINETY-NINE

As the grass blades lean in the wind
I inch toward my wife even in my sleep.
Little things I do unwittingly
develop into a love I have not noticed before.

QUATRAIN ONE HUNDRED

As I have lived some ten years with my woman
I must have mixed my flesh with little things around.
Now tied stubbornly to the kite string of living
I go along as if drunk with life, chained to life.

QUATRAIN ONE HUNDRED AND TWENTY-TWO

On the edge of the city wind-driven garbage balloons
up into the air and descends like a flock of pigeons.
As I go on living trivial things take on a
new meaning. I know what home is like.

Song, Sugwŏn (1940-)

Born in Kohŭng, South Chŏlla, Song received training in creative writing at
Sorabol Arts College. He came to be duly recognized as a poet in 1975 when he
won the New Poet Prize from *Munhak Sasang* (Literature and Thought) and his
epic poem "The Tonghak Uprising" again won him the Prize of the Minister of
Culture and Information. Again in 1986 he received Kumho Literature Award. *At a
Temple Gate*, a selection of his work, came out in 1980. Currently Song teaches at
a local high school.

A SKETCH

A chicken trots behind a ray of sunshine.
Light is being spilt around a drop or two.
A mass of Spanish needles has sprung to
life from where they died last year.
Under a flat floor-stone coated with dry moss
a toad rolls its big eyes.
At that moment a hawk wheeling in the blue
of spring sky falls like a bolt
and snatches off the prey in his crooked hands.
Then the light driven around explodes in mid-air.
And spring looses a flame of heat-waves
from the ridge of the blue-tiled housetop.

AT A TEMPLE GATE

My sister,
Can you see still alive a few hairs of eyebrow
fallen in the shadow of autumn mountain?
The river of millenial nights rearing its head
as I stone-crush to death the undefiled tears
and follow the tear-end.

See every word of suffering settled deep into the waters
come back to stone-life and shine
like a fish leaping into the air?
your gift of a camellia sprig freely offered to the god?

My sister,
Can you see alive the eyebrow
drift about in the shadow of autumn mountain
the eyebrow a wild goose on the wing has shed onto the river?
I drink a cup and another one I offer to thee.
Perhaps, we are to meet again like those water-drops sparkling
on the leaf.

My sister,
Do you know that the few hairs of eyebrow
adrift in the shadow of autumn mountain
now show in the blue waters?

THE CUCKOO ON MT. CHIRI*

Many a cuckoo in many a mountain peak
was crying 'cuckoo,'
'cuckoo' in a body;
it wasn't until thrice three springs
passed, leaving me seasoned with sorrow,
that many a cuckoo turned out
to be a single one.

A single cuckoo
hiding down the side of Mt. Chiri
uttered a cry,
which the next peak echoed
and again echoed the peak after the next
until it seemed many a cuckoo was crying
in a body.

I saw that the chain of mountain peaks
was gradually settling still
the cuckoo's crying gone,
when a silent river started to flow.

I saw that the Sŏmjin River
rolling down in mighty waves
lap the shores of many an isle
that dots the south sea.

I saw the cuckoo crying on a livelong spring day,
down the side of Mt. Chiri, as if drained of its tears
remained to this world remembered as the last sorrowful hues
in which glow the azaleas on the pebbles.

* The name of a mountain some 6,300 feet high bordering the three southern
provinces: Chŏllanamdo, Chŏllabukdo, and Kyŏngsangnamdo.

Yi, Sŏngbu (1942-)

Born in Kwangju, South Chŏlla, Yi studied Korean literature at Kyunghee University. His recognition as a poet came in 1962 when his first poems were published in *Hyondae Munhak* (Modern Literature). His work includes *Poems* (1969), *Our Food* (1974) and *A Trip to the Paekche Dynasty* (1977). Currently, he works for a newspaper in Seoul.

THE BULLDOZER

The hill is jostled at dawn.
One shoulder blade torn off from each
the bleeding bodies are jostled;
jostled again and again until they are
piled into another hill of challenge.
All night long
the faces of men who left their will by suicide,
the minds of men who have endured inner anger,
are jostled together to make for another hill,
a breath steaming from where the hill has been razed,
energy wriggles alive though chopped to pieces.
Still warm,
still generous
it never hates anybody,
big chunks of its flesh ripped apart.
Watch the other hill whose mighty weight
can hardly be jostled, the huge grave.
Listen to the withering word which prompts
warm affection by death.
How can it be removed to another country?
How can tens of thousands of truckloads of earth
get rid of it?

SPRING

You come, unwaited;
come when waiting is forgotten.
Hanging around a nook in the plains
or a stinking puddle,
eyes wandering, waging a fight on the way,
fallen flat exhausted on the ground
and finally shaken awake the wind,
gone to the rescue in the emergency,
you get up rubbing your eyes
and you come so late;
so late but come as sure as fate.
You dazzle my eyes I cannot rise to meet you.
I try to shout but my voice goes petrified.
I cannot announce anything in advance.
I barely extend my arms and embrace you.
O brave, who has come triumphant from far!

THE SEA

The sea does not boast.
She already knows all there is to know.
She repeatedly abides its own whelming power
and repeatedly conceals it.
When fallen, her mind gets renewed,
The mind born in the beginning of time
races on the red cry left behind.
The sea does not speak first.
The sea does not love first.

The sea dies
because it is more beautiful to be in its grave.
The sea sinks blue blade into her breast.

PADDIES

Paddies lean against each other
for survival.
The hotter the sun gets
the sooner they mature;
out of self-love
each leaves itself to its neighbor's care.

The nation grows stronger
when every part is bound to the whole.
Let us imagine those minds boiling with fury
when charged guilty when innocent.
When the paddies start dancing
they vanish in silence.

Paddies know how to keep fit,
washing their sad eyes in the autumn sky;
they hide their own anger
in a breath of wind.
They know their heart is warm.

The bounty of this love
left to us by the paddies as a parting gift,
this heartfelt longing left to us
as they fall and fall only to rise,
the bounty of this strength.

Kim, Yŏn'gyun (1942-   )

Born in Kimje, North Chŏlla, Kim studied creative writing at Sorabol Arts College. He established himself as a poet with his first poems coming out in literary magazines in 1971. Currently, he works as chief editor for a publishing house. He has four books of poems to his credit: *Rainy Season* (1974), *The Seagull* (1977), *The Sea and Children* (1979) and *Man* (1983).

THIS SIDE OF THE GRAVE

I'll be right back.
What do we call the interstice
between the roads, between the stones
between the leaves; the splitting crevice
outside the door in which there's no boundary?
Word forwarded brings
no word back.
No wall in sight,
what are we expected to know,
baffled as if to count hairs?
This side of the grave hymns years and months
which drain away as so much water.
A tear stands out in a blood-stream.
Tears, whither are you streaming?
Where are you going to stop?
I'll be right back.
How much blood should I shed
before a path opens?
I'll be right back,
my blood sprinkled all night long,
opening a road.
I'll be back after staying there a dozen of years.

MESSAGE

Time passes
We pass kneeling down on the road
The unending flow of the mind of treasured things
passes and so does love
The burgeoning wind that has knocked yesterday down
the fiery wind that billows up to vanish
rises again
like a seed leaf opening bud.
Vanity vanity
All is vanity.
When I pass away on a far-off day
or my trace flowers into shimmering air
remember me how I have lived grieving
over my eventual loss
how I have passed away
grieving over my own loss

Remember me. Remember me.

RETURNING HOME

There's no one
But those now returning home.

The wind sways only the budding sprouts;
Along the road hurried crowd surged down;
we go as will those to be born again
and so does love.

All return home down the road
taken by all.

There's no one.
No one dares to beat now
against the currents
for the exploration of a new path.

YEARS AND MONTHS

Who knows?
A man fallen flat in the furrow of time
turns to tears, an embittered spirit
that hovers unable to reach the grave
over this world like shiftless sleet
dampening the ditch.

Who knows?
We, who swarm onto time's wind,
onto time's grass land,
will be gone
scatter away
as when leaves drop with autumn coming;
Father, as when you left me for good.

Years and months, as I watch them,
a grass flower opening at dawn
Prompts my tears, prompts my tears.

Park, Chech'ŏn (1945-)

Born in Seoul, Park went to Dongguk University which he left without earning a degree. At present he works for the Korean Arts and Culture Foundation. He established himself as a poet in 1966 when his first poems were published in *Hyondae Munhak* (Modern Literature). He received several poetry prizes. His work includes *On Changtzu* (1975), *Mind Law* (1979), *Rule* (1981) and *The Third Star* (1983).

MIND, ITS HISTORY

Born only to be trodden
common weeds crop up here and there.
Muted water finds its voice again
while turning a bend in the flow.
I watch the countless stars rise as usual
in rivalry with one another.
Perched precariously on a tree-top
the bird in Paitaishan-ryen's* picture,
only its sight closed up, gaze blankly at them;
gaze far on a road ten thousand leagues ahead.

* A famous painter of the Ch'ing dynasty, China.

DISTRUST

Better not to be born; to die is to suffer.
Do not quite life; to be born again is to suffer.
This is what Christ said.
Life and death alike are suffering,
our old masters said it more briefly.
It is futile to tell life from death.
Who could leave his presence behind and who else would
regain it?
It is also ridiculous for a mere grass
to remark about this or that.

CHANGTZE -33-

Every orbit in heaven is furrowed into a rose-garden.
My lifetime is dressed in a robe of wind.
The way is open on karma's knife-blade
that strikes off rose-sprigs as it comes and goes.
O currents of my blood fleeing into the wind.
O rose-petals blown off in the wind.

HARE HUNTING -13-

I was burning; volumes of smoke
belching out of my body blurred my sight.
Seen from far away a ball of leaping fire
was rolling down an empty field.
For some time the growing field and the growing
fire were battling with each other.
A match stick, lit into charcoal
or reduced to ashes at a mere touch,
I was burning.

HEAVENLY TRAVELER
        -Tu Fu-

What if I should go deaf and sleepless when, old, I quit
    drinking?
Then let me pick up a monkey's chatter in the wind.
I would stay awake overnight pondering over the leaves that
    fall in the distance.
I would follow the sound of water fading at a bend.
I would be flying as a heavenly traveler and think of the white
    hairs beneath my ears.
In the whirligig of life, I would die watching a wild goose's cold
    legs.

Kang, Ŭn'gyo (1945-   )

Born in Seoul, Kang graduated from Yonsei University where she majored in English. She established herself as a poet with her prize-winning piece a *Pilgrim's Sleep* published in *Sasanggye* (The World of Thoughts). She received a Writer's prize in 1975. Her work includes *Nothingness* (1971), *Grass Leaves* (1974) and *A Diary of the Poor* (1977).

IN THE EMPTY SKY AT DUSK

The bright moon walks
to where someone has fallen asleep
and puts down a thin sound
of a stream

The sound of a stream
in turn puts down
a couple of the sea sounds
which are seething inside it

add adds three more sounds,
making them five in all:

one heading to the cliff,
another plummeting from the cliff
and a third digging its own grave under the cliff

leaving the bright guillotined head
suspended alone
in the empty sky at dusk

ROTATION (1)

The day draws to a close.
Far empty fields fall down.
Winds folded in the savannah of sky,
man flutters all by himself.
Houses in the street gently ripple.
The last ray of the sun
is pulling the city God knows where to.

The day draws to a close.
Day in day out fair girls of the land
fall and pile in heaps;
while asleep they are in a hurry,
grains of sand running endlessly
from off their beds.
In the light of many dark centuries
of life-and-death
no one can hide his skin
that peels off one layer after another.

Houses begin to sob.
The day draws to a close.
A life-time sways, wind-locked,
like a falling fruit.
Secretly hanging on every rooftop
the ticking of the clock of the wide sky,
how the girls of sand
pile up in the wasteland!

We left behind us
the longest shadow
as we fell apart.

SHOULD WE EVER BE WATER

Should we ever be water and meet each other
Every droughty household would greet us in glee.
Should we stand side by side with tall trees
and run like rain stampeding in torrents;

Should we run on and on till at dusk
we settle in the deepening waters
soaking the dried-up roots of trees;
Should we ever reach the shy maiden sea . . .

But what we are destined to do is
meet each other as fire;
a black charred bone is already
things of the world on fire.

My sweet that waits ten thousand miles away,
we will be meeting each other
in the wake of the consuming fire.
And uttering the words of fire dying in a hiss,
come to the clear, immense spread of skies
void of any trace of man.

Hŏ, Hyŏngman (1945-   )

Born in Sunchŏn, South Chŏlla Province, Hŏ graduated from Chonnam University where he studied Korean literature. He did graduate work at Sungjon University. His recognition as a poet came in 1973 when his first poems were published in *Wŏlgan Munhak* (Monthly Literature). He has three books of poems to his credit: *Clear Day* (1978), *Grass Leaf Says to God* (1984) and *Lifting a Mosquito Net* (1985). Currently, Hŏ teaches at Mokpo College.

WHERE YOU WISHED ME

I stay where you wished me to.
Remembering your word that
you would not be long
I stand up to the swaying winds
for the far-off days when we'll meet again.

I stay where you wished me to.
Since you went away, I have held on
to this thread of life more short-lived
than a mote of dust, standing up
to the driving rains and winds
only for our solid reunion.

I stay where you wished me to.
From early morning prayer
till midnight hymns
I stand up to the whirling dust,
weary and sad at times,
for the day when you will arrive.

I stay where you wished me to.
Remembering your word that
you would not be long
I stand up to the swaying winds
for the far-off days when we'll meet again.

WINTER SOUND

Trampled
time and again
we will rise propped up
by our faith in greening.

We will rise
and sing in a loud voice
braced up by our hope
for taking firm root in the oncoming spring.

We will call and call
till tears gather in our eyes,
the bitter tears fresh from the heart
because of our love that breaks loose the frozen soil.

There, come and trample us.
Though upsurging pain
whips us into whisps of grass,
we will rise time and again
and sing in a loud voice
till we break down
and turn into a star in heaven.

FOR THE POOR

Frail in the blade,
yet tenacious in the roots,
grass sways in the winds;
it keeps to its own ground.
Fixed in its own place
grass sobs inwardly.
Tonight as usual
it lights a lamp and tends it.
Rejoice in the winds
for they will make it strong.
All those who are poor,
let not your poverty
bring you low and humble
the way grass never feels sorry
for its grassiness.

SNOWFALL ON THE SEAS

Oh, you have gone, my friend, leaving me
standing on the shore of Mokpo*
from which I watch the snow fall
thick and fast on the coastal seas
in a glitter like your departed spirit.
On the calm sea the snow
dissolves as it descends.
What song do you want me to sing
when I cannot so much whistle, jaws-viced, tongue-tied?
Oh, you have gone, my friend, leaving me
all alone. I know no one is free
from worldly cares and pains.
I watch from this shore the snow
swirling in midair in a glitter
like your departed spirit,
falling thick and fast
on the coastal seas
under my eyes.

* A port city in the south.

Moon, Chunghee (1947-   )

A native of Posŏng, South Chŏlla Province, Moon studied Korean at Tongguk University both as an undergraduate and graduate student. She took courses at new York University for two years as a non-degree student. A succession of her early poems came out in *Wolgan Munhak* (Monthly Literature) in 1969. In 1975 she was awarded the Modern Literature Prize. She has to her credit eight volumes of poems: *Flower's Breath* (1969), *Collected Poems* (1973), *Bell-sound Falling on its Own* (1984), *My Brother's Bird* (1986), *My Sweet Home* (1987), *The Wild Rose* (1987), *You're Gone Farther than the Sky* (1988) and *To Young Love* (1991), selected poems.

POEM AT FORTY

The number seems more honest than the poem.
Turning forty today
skin in the neck firm and bouncy till yesterday at thirty nine
has grown limp and flabby overnight,
into a waste mass of cotton wool.

At a funeral strewn
with yellow chrysanthemums
I see myself framed in the place
of the dead person's photograph,
finding myself lamenting over my own death.

I get cross when I have no reason to.
I get scared for no reason whatsoever.
I start forgetting to love
rather than make a cowardly effort
to love anew.

What is it to be forty?
All shades of gray on earth
hovering overhead so far
now settles in me, into my whole being
and I feel like dialing phone numbers
anywhere to order a new dress made for me.

How a mere number crushes my spirit
into a wilted flower on the grass!

LETTER
—for my 78-year mother at home awaiting death—

Love only one thing
leaving all else into forgetfulness.

I do not mean it is a life
to be dearly held on to
but I mean it should be a promise to keep.

Each of us is heading lonely
for the same destination.
This is a pleasant promise, Mother.

You'll be leaving a little earlier, Mother
as an early comer should.

And we must follow you a little later
as late comers should.

We come into the world without a promise
but we have promises to keep on our way.
It isn't that lonely to leave;
why should you cry, Mother?

You've been a lovely leaf, now falling.

A SONG

Even if your sorrow, my dearest love,
should run like a rolling river,

Even if my white prayer should ride
on the sunbeam and plays round your ears like a wind,

I could never enter your dreams
nor can you ever get mine open.

Even if we should love each other to the utmost.

A FLOCK OF BIRDS

Is the river alone flowing, I wonder?
Blood too flows into the heaven,
so heavenward do the fallen leaves,
unaware where they are from;
each serving as its own road,
as a point of departure.

Sleepless hours stubborn to the end,
smudged in dots on the face,
like a howling light,
O love that soars forever!
Following in your wake
all of us flow together
heading forever heavenward
with no cause to cry.

Kim, Namju (1946-1994)

A native of Haenam, South Chŏlla Province, Kim was admitted to Chonnam National University in 1968 but was soon forced to leave because of his political activism. As a student, he edited an underground newspaper "Outcry" in a move to oppose the dictatorial rule. Since 1973 his life has been spent in on-and-off imprisonment. Again in 1988 he was sentenced to 15 years and was released on parole in 1988 on the strength of petitions by writers at home and International P.E.N. members. His first collected poems *Requiem* came out in 1984, followed by *My Sword and My Blood* (1987), *My Country is One* (1988), *Love's Weapon* (1989), *Let's Speak Out* (1989) and *The Abode of Ideas* (1992). Kim's work as a whole is strongly tinged with ideological protest against capitalistic exploitation.

THIS AUTUMN

This autumn, in a blue prison uniform, hands tied behind my back, feet in manacles, I am taken to another part of the country. Where am I being carried now, I wonder, to Chonju Jail or Kwangju or somewhere else? My jail van runs out of the crowded street of a familiar city onto the middle of fields. I wish to get off here from the coop and to head to my mother who is picking peppers in the field with a hot sun on her back, to join my father who is harvesting in the paddy-field bending his newly-sharpened sickle, and to play with the children who form a circle on the bank urging sheep to horn each other for a fight. I wish to get off free from ropes and chains. I wish to run freely with my son our arms spread out skyward.
I wish to run till my ankles grow numb in the paddy path;
I wish to run with the wind blowing full in my breast;
I wish to run till I grow out of breath.
When thirsty, I'll cup my hands to drink from a roadside spring-well; when hungry, I will pull out a radish by the roots beside the road and feed on it along the endless road I take, and when tired at the close of the day I will head homeward the way homing birds do.
But the prison car never stops but continues on its way crossing field after field. Now it is crossing the historic river on which farmers rose up a long time ago to fight the corrupt government; the farmer-militia defeated the nobles and rich as they advanced on this hilly pass to seize the provincial capital. I am crossing the same pass, the old battle site. This autumn, in a blue prison uniform . . .

SPRING IN THE HILLS AND FIELDS

Someone asked me in passing:
"Where is he now?"
He's gone there, I said.

Where is there? he raised a query
pointing to a white-washed building behind the wall
where liberty writhes to shake off the bondage.

On arrival of spring in the hills and fields
someone asked me in passing:
Hasn't he been freed yet?
Pointing to a grave
I answered he is there now.

A VIRGIN BOY AND A VIRGIN GIRL

A comely young girl
surrendered her chastity
to a gigolo-like playboy
out of her sheer vanity.

A youth as innocent as possible
lost his innocence to a whore
near Seoul Station or in a brothel
somewhere in the city.

At acertain day and hour and in a certain month of a certain year
they met as a cherry boy and a cherry girl;
at a certain day and hour in a certain month of a certain year
they were coupled by an officiator
at a wedding ceremony. And so the story goes.

Cho, Chŏnggwŏn (1949-)

A native of Seoul, Cho graduated from the English Education Department of Chung'ang University. He made his debut as a poet through recommendation of Mogwŏl Park in 1970, when his poems were accepted by *Hyondae Shihak* (Modern Poetics). His books of poems include *Seven Types of Mind Looking at Rain* (1977), *Poems* (1982), *Ode on the Open Mind* (1985), *Heaven Quilt* (1987) and *The Mountaintop Graveyard* (1991). He was awarded a couple of literary prizes. Currently he works for the Korea Culture and Arts Foundation.

THE MOUNTAINTOP GRAVEYARD I

Climbing the winter hills I see
the most highminded things in
cold places glitter like ice,
a stern silence of icefall.
The loftiest mind moves alive
in cold places, singing of
a freeze of every rock in every ravine
that cracks white in the act of freezing.
The mountaintop
mantled in masses of ice
is holding up light.
Should my soul ever dream of a celestial castle
I would long for a niche of God-dwelling heaven.
The loftiest mind is made for the coldest place.
What flows far below isn't going to freeze
but prefers to maintain silence.

Things that move will never be stilled hence
but join the silence in a song of silence.
But this spirit once sunk to sleep
will not rouse from its perfect rest
unless whipped hard with a stick.
Likewise, one form
will not turn into another form
unless whipped by somebody.
Flesh is nothing but tatters,
futile rests and days of wandering in a sleep.
Should my soul make no
loud clapping of its hands

in the middle of silence,
I would never dream again of taking any form.
This is a season for freezing. During the night
shore and sea will pull each other, singing
a song of freezing under my feet.

All summer long
fascinated with their own force
streams of water that thundered in the valleys
down the tumbling falls are frozen over.
Chunks of ice lying flat
in every ravine
are fascinated with their own force.
O wind for freezing,
blow, whirling
into my vessels.
From top to toe
penetrate my spirit;
occupy and
intoxicate it.
The birds on the mountaintop
brooding on the bare tree-tops
dream of moments of ecstasy, their wings folded;
wild fruits are shrunk to a few dry seeds,
intoxicated inside their skins.
The roots kissing raindrops all
summer long, now by the frozen rocks
are biting into earth, fascinated with their own teeth
and rocks drunk with their own dead weight
tremble in their own delight.

Look, how the rocks are fascinated
by their own load on the backs!
Yet skies are innumerable breasts held up in the void.
A host of breasts vanishing into the void
and crowds of wrists supporting candlelights
must be climbing the staircase of naked tree
showered down with bliss of light.
Strewing on each heavenly staircase
a fire-flower that contains pure and clean seeds,

my eyes must have dreamt of the hour of intoxication.
Wasn't it that my hours were sinking
weighed down by the heaviness of dazzling maturity?
Night, give orders for mobilization.
Come closer and closer
to occupy and overwhelm
my blood vessels and my bones;
penetrate them.

Once, darkness approached me daily in the form of rain and snow;
It would approach me daily in the form of wind;
and then in the form of fire and water.
In that darkness were a futile rest and prolonged wait.
Didn't I meet the sleepless nights
of the exhausted minds with my daily gravity?
Darkness is a green wood's scent sprayed over the abode of being.
How I wished my soul to be soaked in its scent!
How I have dreamed of the white night
when my soul brings me my own blessing!
Flesh is nothing but tatters that blown off by the wind
unless soul keeps it down with a weight.

THE MOUNTAINTOP GRAVEYARD 19

We are all flesh born
and stranded on the earth.

In a die-hard reach for an unattainable height
species of man lie stretched on their backs
on the winter ground that spews frost from its storage of cold.

One day in the early spring you ran into a newly-dug grave.

A grass scent that assailed you
was an excuse for us to live out to the end.

THE MOUNTAINTOP GRAVEYARD 22

Rain falls on the ground; snow on the mountaintop.
Why is snow shy of descending to the ground?
Because it wishes to keep its pure crane-like
mind hidden high on the mountaintop?

SEALED-UP AUTUMN

Faraway skies get sere and sallow.

Leaves fall from the trees.
From the trees leaves fall.
Joined hands forgive.

Autumn is here and I have only myself to seek.

Hence I shall be an apple-tree
and must write poems far into the night
on the apple leaves spread on my desk.

Unmistakably.

Hence I shall be an apple-tree
and must write poems brightened up
by the burnished fruit loading the boughs.

INDEX OF POETS*

* In romanizing proper names, personal names in particular, the author has adopted the McCune-Reischauer transcription system. And so personal names can differ from the ones actually used. However, exceptions are made of some names preferred by the poets. And also following the general practice *Park* is preferred to *Pak* but *Yi* is employed for *Lee* or *Rhee*. In some cases, pen names are more common than real names, for instance: Ansŏ Kim is the pen name for Ŏk Kim; Jonggil Kim for Ch'igyu Kim; Sowŏl Kim for Chongshik Kim; Yuksa Yi for Hwal Yi and Sang Yi for Haegyŏng Kim. It is also important to note that family names come first in Korea and at times family names are used in capital letters without a comma after them.

Index of Titles

A

B

C

D

G

H

I

K

L

M

N

Q

R

S

DATE DUE

JUL 0 9 1992			
OCT 1 0 1998			
JAN 24 2006			
			Printed in USA

HIGHSMITH #45230